Imagine That!

Imagine That!

365 Wacky Ways to Build a Creative Christian Family

Mike and Amy Nappa

Augsburg
MINNEAPOLIS

For Sprout and Flash,
and bad movie nights yet to come!

IMAGINE THAT!

365 Wacky Ways to Build a Creative Christian Family

Imagine That! is another creative resource from the authors at Nappaland Communications Inc. To contact the authors, send e-mail to: Nappaland@aol.com.

Cover illustrations by Stephanie Roth
Cover design by Marti Naughton
Text design by James Satter

Library of Congress Cataloging-in-Information Data

Nappa, Mike, 1963-
    Imagine that!: 365 wacky ways to build a creative Christian family
Mike and Amy Nappa
    p. cm.
    ISBN 0-8066-3618-1 (alk. paper)
    1. Family—Religious life. 2. Family recreation. I. Nappa, Amy,
1963- . II. Title.
BV4526.2.N36   1998   98-10850
249—dc21   CIP

The paper used in this publication meets the minimum requirements of American National Standard for Information Sciences—Permanence of Paper for Printed Library Materials, ANSI Z329.48-1984.

Manufactured in the U.S.A.   AF 9-3618

02   01   00   99   98   1   2   3   4   5   6   7   8   9   10

INTRODUCTION

You May Not Have Noticed This, But . . .

We serve an infinitely creative God. This is the Person who created the giraffe, the ant, puppies, thunderstorms, solar systems, children, volcanoes, beaches, emus, snow, Hawaii, Antarctica, grasshoppers, camels (one hump, or two?), and you.

You may not have noticed this, but . . . God placed in you a flicker of the same creativity that he used to make the universe. Burning inside your mind, deep in the heart of your very being is the image of God—the image of the One who began this whole universe by being creative.

You may not have noticed this, but . . . your life doesn't have to be boring. Your days don't have to be one monotonous 24-hour period after another. Your relationships don't have to be "just the same old stuff." Your town doesn't have to be "too small" or "too big" or "too" anything. After all, you are a part of something creative.

Perhaps it's time for you to stop and take notice of God's creativity that surrounds your entire life. You can use this book to help you do that. Go ahead, we don't mind. In fact, that's why we wrote it in the first place.

So What's in This Book Anyway?

In the pages that follow, you'll find hundreds of wacky ways you can use to build a creative family. These ideas aren't meant to replace your own creativity, but to inspire, enhance, and bring to the fore your family's God-given innovative abilities.

The ideas in this book come directly out of our own lives and experiences. Since we earn our living by being creative, we can't afford to let the light of our creativity grow dim! So, we regularly look for opportunities to feed the flame God has put within us. We've discovered that our creative energies are fed when we:

- change our perspective,
  - challenge our thinking,
    - encourage risk-taking,
      - expand our boundaries, and
        - experience something out of the ordinary.

7

So, we've collected our favorite ideas and put them in this book for you and your family to share. And because creativity doesn't have an age limit, we've included ideas from each member of our family—parent and child alike.

A Few Things to Remember . . .

• Feel free to browse. One of the great things about a book like this is that you don't have to read it from start to finish. You can start in the middle, skip to the end, jump back to the beginning and still get what you need. So, go ahead and do it! Find the ideas that grab your attention right away and try those out first. Then you can go back and try other wacky ways that might be fun for you and your family.

• Be willing to risk. Don't immediately dismiss an idea because it seems a stretch for you. Sometimes it's those out-of-your-comfort-zone types of experiences that bring the brightest flashes. Remember, God sometimes uses discomfort to light the dawn of realization. (Don't believe it? Check out what God did with Jonah, Balaam, and Peter. You'll find their stories in the Bible, in Jonah 1-4, Numbers 22, and Matthew 14:22-33, respectively.)

• Be aware that not every idea is perfect for everyone—and that's OK. For instance, if you're a professional harmonica player, creative spark # 96 ("Learn a Song on the Harmonica") might not make a big impact for you. If an idea doesn't seem just right for you or your family, don't be afraid to adapt it to better fit your lifestyle and interests. (How about a new song on the kazoo?)

• This book is worthless unless you *use* it. We'll be honest. We hate books that just sit on a shelf. We didn't write *Imagine That!* to be a book you skim through, chuckle at possibilities, comment to your spouse, "We ought to try this sometime," and then file away. We wrote this book to be used, to be mangled, to have its binding torn off because of repeated opening and shutting, to be handled by children, teenagers, and adults, to be a conversation-starter for those who witness you engaging a creative spark, and . . . well, you get the idea.

With every activity we've included a short prayer—a quick way to connect with our creative God. So what are you waiting for? Turn the page and start the adventure. Once you do, maybe you'll notice something you never noticed before.

Mike and Amy Nappa

1
Play with a Preschooler

Let the child pick the game. As you play, ask yourself: "What captures the imagination of this child? What does this child see with ease that I must strain to see? What can I do today to dream with the imagination of a child? Ask God to give you the eyes of a child as you walk down the path this week takes you.

Lord, give me the eyes of a child as I walk down the path that this week will take me.

2
Read the Sunday Comics from the Past Year

Go to your local library and ask for the microfiche archives of the Sunday paper for your area. Then spend time reading (or rereading) all your favorite Sunday comics on microfiche. Take note of what makes you laugh and what doesn't. Afterward, pray for the ability to see and appreciate the humorous moments to come over the next 12 months.

Jesus, grant me the ability to see and appreciate the humorous moments in this life.

3
Create a New Dessert—Just for You!

Gather your five favorite sweets, then begin experimenting to find the best way to combine all five sweets into one super-duper dessert. For example, you might stick a candy bar into a slice of cheesecake, sprinkle it with jelly beans, crumble carrot cake into fudge sauce, and pour the sauce over the whole concoction. If the other members of your family are nice, go ahead and offer to share with them.

Lord, help me not to gain too much weight from today's little experiment!

4

Drive (or Walk) to Work (or School) a Completely Different Way

Be sure to allow extra time for this—you may need it! Pull out a map of your area, and plot a course to work or school that takes you by someplace you've never (or rarely) been. That may mean driving away from your destination in order to get there! As you pass by the scenery on your new route, ask yourself: Why don't I come to this area more often? What's one thing I'd have missed out on if I hadn't taken this route today?

Jesus, show me the ways to serve you that I've never been able to see before.

5

Write a Beginning and Ending for Someone Else's Middle

Find a children's picture book and photocopy a page from the middle. (Dr. Seuss books are especially fun for this activity!) Staple two blank sheets of paper to the photocopied page—one sheet before and one sheet after the photocopied page. The result will be a mini-book with a blank beginning and a blank ending. When you're ready, work together as a family to create a new beginning and write it on the front page. (Include illustrations if you like!) Then create a new ending for the back page. Now, read the new story with your beginning, the original middle, and your new ending. If you like it, do a sequel!

God, help us to revel in the joy that comes from a new beginning in you, and take comfort in knowing you've taken care of the endings in our life stories.

Mike and Amy Nappa

6

Lie on Your Back and Look at the Evening Sky

If possible (and safe), climb on your roof while you do this. See
how far you can focus your vision (be careful not to look directly
in the sun, though!). Take a moment to ponder that the daylight
you see and feel started 93,000,000 miles away from where you are
right now. Count the number of colors you see in the sky. Think
of how far away the sun and the other stars are. Afterward, ask
family members: What kind of creativity must God have to make
this sky? How do I benefit from God's creative power? How can I
share in that creative power this week?

God, thank you for being creative, for being you.

7

Tie Your Shoelaces Backwards

Relace your shoes so that they tie at the toes instead of the ankles.
Then go about your day as normal. See how long it takes for you
to become used to the fact that your laces are backward. See if anyone around you notices and asks about your laces. Make plans to
change one small thing about yourself tomorrow as well.

*Lord, show me the small changes you want me to make in my
life this week.*

8

Pray in a Closet

Go ahead, conquer that claustrophobia and close the door. While
your eyes adjust to the dark, take time to remember that God sees
everything around you, and miraculously hears the thoughts your
mind whispers to God in prayer. When you finish your prayer
time, ask yourself: How did being in a closet change my perspective on prayer? my prayer itself?

Jesus, teach me to pray today.

9

Read a Dictionary

You'd be surprised the kinds of thing we have words for in the English language! For example, if you need a word for "resembling a limpet," you can use "pateliform." Have everyone look through pages of the dictionary to spot the most unusual sounding word or words with the wackiest definitions. Then try to combine everyone's choices to make one complete (if slightly zany!) sentence.

Lord, let us use a new word (or two!) to praise you today.

10

Read Your Bible Upside-down

Not getting a lot out of your Bible reading lately? Try approaching it from different angle—literally! Turn your Bible upside down and read an entire chapter that way. Pay attention to the kinds of adjustments you make to enable you to read. Afterward, ask yourself: In what ways is my current relationship with God "upside down"? What kind of adjustments do I need to make to get it right again?

God, give me a new perspective this week on how to apply your Word in my life.

11

Wear Every Piece of Jewelry You Own

Gather all the family's jewels (from Mom's diamond ring to the littlest one's friendship bracelet) and select one person to be a model. Then, working as a team, place every piece of jewelry your family owns on that person. You may need to make creative use of space, like putting earrings in button holes, or making necklaces into anklets. Afterward, take a picture of your model to remember the results of this silly spark!

Jesus, show us how to "wear" your righteousness like fine jewelry this week.

12
See How Many Layers of Clothes You Can Wear

Make it a contest. Send every family member to his or her room to put on as many layers of clothes as possible—piling on T-shirts, sweatshirts, shorts, jeans, and even sweaters and winter coats. After 15 minutes, have family members emerge and compare outfits. Award a family hug to the person with the most layers. (Note: This spark works particularly well during the winter when everyone is begging to turn up the thermostat!)

Father, help us feel the warmth of your love in special ways this week.

13
Give Yourself a "Most Likely to . . ." Award

Take a page from a high-school senior's yearbook and vote yourself "Most Likely to . . ." something. Instead of things like "Most Likely to Succeed" or "Most Likely to Become a Movie Star," give you and your family members important awards. For example, "Most Likely to Win a Tickle Fight" or "Most Likely to Eat a Whole Pizza by Himself" or "Most Likely to Make Others Smile." When everyone is ready, hold an awards ceremony in the living room, using Twinkies™ as the trophies.

Jesus, grant that we may be "Most Likely to Imitate You Today."

14
Display Your Ignorance of the World of Cyberspace

Join an on-line chat that's discussing a topic you know absolutely nothing about. Ask stupid questions until you feel like you have a better understanding of what they're talking about and why they feel like it's worth discussing. Then impress your coworkers and friends with your newfound knowledge!

Lord, help me understand your will for my life.

15
Smile in Public

Believe it or not, most Americans are conditioned to scowl in public. Next time you're driving on the freeway, try smiling at the driver who passes you. Flash a grin to a person passing you as you enter a store. Look for opportunities to share a smile in a day—and watch how people react. Some will be surprised, some will ignore you, and a few may even smile back!

Loving Spirit, allow us to share our smiles with the people who need them today.

16
Build the Ultimate Paper Airplane

You'll want to have several sheets of paper handy for this one. First decide what would make a paper airplane "ultimate." Is it flying distance? Height achieved? Speed from point A to point B? Simple good looks? After you've decided, begin experimenting with new designs until you've created that one model that you can confidently declare is The Ultimate Paper Flying Machine!

Jesus, show me what it means to be the "ultimate" follower of you.

17
Sponsor a Tabletop Football Tournament

Clean off your dining room table, fold a few paper footballs, invite over your friends, and stage the first official tabletop football tournament at your house. Play in round-robin fashion, and declare the first person to reach 25 points in each game as that game's winner. (Of course, like any football game, you'll need an abundance of junk food and soft drinks!) Award the person with the most victories a hallowed "Whatever Junk Food Is Left Over" award.

In case you're not acquainted with this lunchroom sport, here's how you play. First, to create the "ball" fold a sheet of paper into thirds, then into a triangle shape. Set a player on each side of a table, then have players take turns flicking the ball back and forth. To score a touchdown, flick so the ball hangs slightly over an opponent's table edge—without falling off. If a player knocks the ball off the table three times between scores, the opposing player get to attempt a field goal, worth three points. For kicks—extra points and field goals—the defensive player touches his or her index finger tips and raises thumbs to form goal posts, while the offensive player flicks the ball airborne through the goal post thumbs to score.

God, help me to reflect you in both the thrill of life's victories, and the agonies of life's defeats.

18
Celebrate an Un-Birthday

Pick a day on which no one in your family has a birthday—and throw an un-birthday party! Don't forget streamers, cake, ice cream, and silly party games like Pin the Tail on the Donkey (or its variation—"Tape the Tail on Dad!"). Watch Disney's *Alice in Wonderland* to wind down afterward.

Thank you, Jesus, for being born into our world.

19
Make a List of "Things to Do Before I Die"

Give some thought to what you want to accomplish and get out of life, then make a list of things you want to complete before you die. Include everything you want to do, no matter how big or small. (When we did this, the number one item on both our lists was "Visit Walt Disney World!") Want to write a book? bungee jump? run a marathon? record a song? be in a movie? own your own business? meet your favorite actor? Take some time to dream. Then figure out ways to make those dreams come true before you die.

God, make it my life's desire to accomplish all that you desire.

20

Title Your Biography

Imagine they've written a book about your life to date, and now the publisher has asked you to title it. What phrase summarizes your life so far? If you're a child, you might call your book, *Your Face Will Freeze Like That! and Other Threats My Parents Used on Me*. A teenager might use the title, *So Much Schoolwork, So Little Time*. Think of titles that are both humorous and serious—but always true somehow.

Thank you, Jesus for "titling" your life with love.

21

Decide Who Plays Who in the Movie of Your Family's Life

Once they write a book about you, a movie is the next logical step, right? Decide who should play each of your family members when they make that blockbuster thriller about your life. In fact, pick two or three stars to play you—one person is just not good enough! (For our family, we've decided on Brad Pitt, Sandra Bullock, and Eric Lloyd.)

Lord, teach us to trust you even when we aren't sure what'll happen next in the "plot" of our lives.

22

Mail Yourself a Letter

Write a letter to your future self, that person who you'll become three or four days from today. Tell yourself all about who you are right now, what you like and dislike, your favorite thing from the day, and anything you want that person to remember (like "go to the store" or "don't forget to hug your spouse"). Mail it and see how much changes in the time it takes for you to receive it.

God, remind us to read (and reread) the letter you sent us, the Bible.

23
Create and Bury a Time Capsule

Collect artifacts from around your house that reveal something about each member of your family, and place everything in a large container. For example, you might include movie ticket stubs, a picture of you in a Halloween costume, a baseball, and so on. Let each family member also add one "secret artifact" that no one else knows about. Then bury the container in the backyard. Dig it up a year later to rediscover the family you once were.

Jesus, allow us to rediscover your love each day this week.

24
Use the Word "Blue" in Every Conversation

Every time you talk to someone during the day, try to slip in the word "blue" somewhere. People might think you're nuts, but that's OK! Encourage your friends to join you in this challenge. See how often you can say "blue" in such a way that nobody notices you've done anything out of the ordinary. (And by the way . . . BLUE!)

Lord, show me your glory in today's blue sky!

25
Search for Something Beautiful

Go on a hunt to find the most beautiful thing around. Perhaps it'll be a butterfly in a park, the smile of a friend, the eyes of your spouse, a new outfit in a store, a picture you've drawn with crayons, the sunset, or a gnarled tree that's perfect for climbing. When you find it, be sure to share it with someone else!

Thank you, Creator God, for giving beauty to this life.

26

Visit a Toy Store

(Warning: We believe it's unethical to take a child into Toys-R-Us and not buy anything! So be prepared to make at least a small purchase.) Now that we've got that out of the way, gather the whole clan on a Saturday morning and explore the aisles of your favorite toy store. Look for the family consensus "Most Fun Toy in America" and be sure to test a few along the way. Brainstorm ways to make homemade imitations of the favorite gadgets you see. Then go home and spend the rest of the day making them!

Jesus, help us treasure the fun moments we have as a family.

27

Sing into a Fan

Warning: Don't do this without parental supervision. Once you've got Mom or Dad in tow, turn on the nearest fan and sing your favorite song into it, listening for the vibrating echo it makes on the fan. ("Row, Row, Row Your Boat" works well for this!) Experiment to see how the sound of your voice changes as you adjust the fan speed, try new songs, imitate your favorite singers, and so on. Keep going until Mom threatens to wrap the fan cord around your neck. (Just kidding!)

Let my voice sing praise to you all the days of my life.

28

Squish Your Toes in the Mud

Find a nice muddy spot, slip off your shoes and socks, and bury your feet in the squishy, mushiness of the mud. (Add water as needed to assure continued squishiness.) Draw designs in the mud with your toes, describe what the mud feels like to each other, and simply enjoy the soft coolness of the mud and the company of your family nearby!

Lord, help us to see your hand in the simple pleasures of life.

29

Finger-Paint

Cover the table with paper, roll up your sleeves, get paint all over your hands, then, using your fingers as paintbrushes, create your most imaginative drawings. How about a pink and green sky? or an orange snowman? or a portrait of God? And remember, it's OK to have fun and get a little messy at the same time!

God, thank you for painting my life with the colors of love.

30

Make Five People Laugh

Tough assignment, but definitely doable! Look for opportunities for bringing a giggle to the lips of at least five people today. Share a funny story, tell a (clean) joke, make a silly face, slip on a banana peel (but don't hurt yourself!), imitate your favorite TV comedian, do whatever it takes to make a laugh. And don't forget, if you laugh, that counts as one person!

Lord, help me find—and share—the joy that comes with knowing you.

31

Read the Headlines from the Day You Were Born

Take a trip to the library and look for newspapers or magazines printed on the dates each family member was born. (You'll probably need to consult the microfiche archives for this.) Spend some time discovering what the world thought was newsworthy on the days you each were born. For extra fun, use construction paper to make your own "Front Page Newspapers" that announce each person's birth as a mega-news event.

Father, let our family be a little good news for someone this week.

32
Make a Chronology of Your Life

Beginning with the first year of life, have each person list one highlight for each year he or she has been alive. For example, "Year 1: Got teeth!" . . . "Year 2: Learned to Walk" . . . "Year 15: Met best friend, Rex Stepp" . . . "Year 22: Joined a Gospel Choir!" and so on. Compare your lists, then invent potential highlights for the next two or three years to come.

Lord, help our family to be a highlight for you today.

33
Throw a Party for
"Yell Fudge at the Cobras in North America" Day

Yes, this is a real day! It falls on June 2 each year (but you can celebrate it anytime). So don't delay, plan your party today! Be sure to include plenty of (what else?) fudge, a few rubber snakes, and all kinds of fudgy-fun games. For more information on this inventive holiday, contact the Wellness Permission League in Mt. Gretna, Pennsylvania.

Thank you, Jesus, for giving us reason to celebrate each and every day.

34
Go Camping in Your Backyard

Grab the tent, sleeping bags, camp rations, and bug spray and head into the backyard for an overnight camping trip. Make everyone promise not to reenter the house under any condition (except to use the bathroom). Light a "campfire" on a grill, cook food, sing songs, make up wild camping adventure stories, and generally enjoy the great outdoors of your backyard.

God, show us how to live to the utmost the lifelong adventure of following you.

35

Read a Recommended Book

Ask several friends to recommend a favorite author and favorite books. From the recommendations you receive, pick an author you've never read, and read one of that person's books. Ask yourself: What made this book and/or this author so appealing to my friend? How is my friend's taste similar to or different from mine? What books would I recommend to others?

Remind me today, Lord, to read the book you recommended—the Bible.

36

Watch *Mary Poppins*

This movie has more imagination than any other 10 movies put together, so rent the video and gather everyone around to watch Bert dance on chimneys, children enter sidewalk drawings, uncles laugh their way to the ceiling, and Mary Poppins make chores into games. Afterward, have everyone answer this question: How would our home change if Mary Poppins came to live here?

Creative Spirit, let my imagination run wild today.

37

Make a Difference for Someone

Look for a unique way to make a positive impact on someone this week. Perhaps you'll be a listening ear for a friend, pay a teenager's way to your church's youth camp, take a child for an outing, assist a coworker on a difficult project, give your spouse a back rub after a long day, or pray for a specific need in your church. The possibilities are endless!

Jesus, make a difference in my life today.

38
Sit in on a College Class

Take your seat to a local seat of learning and get permission to sit in on a class that sounds interesting to you. Pretend you're the professor's supervisor and are there to grade his or her performance. Award points for creative teaching techniques, knowledge of the material, interaction with students, preparation for class time, and any other criteria you feel important. If the professor rates well, consider enrolling in a class in the future.

Spirit of Love, show me how to score an A+ in love today.

39
Play "Celebrity Look-alikes" in the Maternity Ward

Take a trip to your local hospital and get permission to view the babies in the maternity ward. While admiring God's miracles, figure out which celebrities the babies look most like. Is that a Jack Nicholson double over there? Holly Hunter in the corner crib? Mel Gibson crying his lungs out? If you're adventuresome, match the nurses with celebrities, too!

Jesus, help our family to be "look-alikes" of you.

40
Rename Your Family Members for a Day

Admit it—you've all toyed with the idea of having a different name. So why not rename yourselves just for fun, just for your family, and just for a day? Think of names you like (such as Tony or Alexandra), or names that are silly (like Cheese Pizza or Mikeyman), and have each family member choose his or her favorite. Call each other those new names all day long.

Thank you, Father, for allowing our family to be adopted into yours.

41
Eat Lebanese Food

Lebanese is Mike's favorite ethnic food, so make him happy by munching on stuffed grape leaves, kibbe, cabbage rolls, and baklava (check out a Lebanese cookbook from the library to help you). Try at least one thing you've never eaten before, and then describe it in detail to another family member.

God is great, God is good, now let's eat up all this food.

42
Wear a Sling for a Day

We're betting you've taken those arms of yours for granted lately, so it's time for this little experiment. When you get up in the morning, place one arm in a sling (your pick of which arm), and then imagine you're unable to use it the entire day. (Of course, you'll probably want to plan extra time to get ready for school.) At the end of the day, ask yourself: How did not using an arm change my perspective today?

Father, teach me how to walk arm in arm with you each day of my life.

43
Tie-Dye a Shirt

Give everyone a white T-shirt. Have each person twist his or her shirt tightly, and wrap portions of the twisted cloth with rubber bands about one to two inches apart. Next dip the shirts in clothing dye according to manufacturer's directions. Hang shirts up to dry, leaving the rubber bands on. When they're dry, wash in cold water, tumble dry, and admire your creations! (If you're really gutsy, wear them to church next week!)

We praise You, God, 'cause you're the grooviest of all!

44
Design a Web Page about Your Family

Grab a "how-to" book from the library, browse the Internet for ideas, then design a web page that uniquely reflects your family's personality. Make sure everyone has input, and be sure to include "gateway" icons to transport web surfers from your page to related web pages (such as the chocolate lovers paradise, or the rock-n-roll home page!)

Thank you, Creative God, for the unique personality each one of us adds to our family.

45
Read a (Clean) Joke Book

A joke is funny because it surprises us with a new perspective, a play on words, or a silly situation. So grab a joke book and look for surprises! (We like just about anything by Bob Phillips—jokes so corny they're funny!) Be sure to practice your comedic delivery on anyone standing nearby while you read.

Lord, let me laugh at the humor you've planted in my world today.

46
Write a Brand New Knock-Knock Joke

With all the inspiration you gathered from #45, this should be a breeze for you! Here's our humble offering: Knock knock! Who's There? Yah. Yah who? You don't have to cheer, it's just a knock-knock joke! (See, now it's OK if yours is corny, 'cause it can't be as bad as ours!)

Jesus, thank you for being willing to knock at the door of my heart.

47
Invent a Game That Requires Couch Cushions

Couch cushions—they're not just for sitting on anymore. Gather the family, pull off every cushion in the house, and invent a new game that uses them. How about "Cushion Wars"? or "Island Hopping" or "Cushion Armor Gladiators"? Don't just sit there—get bouncing!

Lord, thanks for creating families and fun—and couch cushions.

48
Build a Lego™ Sculpture

Pour out a pile of these unique building blocks and let your imagination run wild. (If you want to cheat, you can buy instructions for specialized, pre-planned sculptures at your local toy store.) Work as a group or individually, to create a tower, a car, or a model of your pet dog. Whatever you do, take time to create.

Help us today, God, to be creative just like you.

49
Make a Tape of Your Top 10 Favorite Songs

You don't need a radio station to tell you what the greatest hits are—you can decide for yourself. Imagine you're a disc jockey whose assignment is to air the 10 best songs ever recorded. Then choose those 10 songs, record them back to back on a cassette tape for your own personal use, and enjoy! (For extra fun, record an introduction to each song in your best DJ voice.)

Thanks, Spirit of Joy, for the gift of music and the power of song.

50
Create a Family Symbol

Brainstorm the best symbol to represent what you want your family to be known for (such as a home in the shape of a cross, or even something silly like a pizza delivery guy stopping at your house). Then call on the talents of an artistic family member or friend to illustrate your family's chosen symbol. Have letterhead, T-shirts, caps, pens, and other fun stuff made that proudly displays your family's symbol. Be ready to explain the symbol to any who ask about it.

Father, help us remember what our family stands for this week.

51

Make Up a Secret, Nonverbal Code for Family Members Only

This will come in especially handy when you're at some social function where talking aloud could be a hindrance. You might want to create signs that mean "This is boring!" "Way to go!" "What fun!" "I'm starving!" "Gotta go to the bathroom!" and (of course) "I love you!"

God, you know all our secrets. Thanks for loving us anyway!

52

Plan a Family Reunion

Of course, you don't have to actually put on a family reunion, but planning one can be gobs-o-fun. First select the ideal spot for your family to get together. Next make a guest list of all the relatives you hope would come. Brainstorm fun activities. Plan the perfect menu for your time together, and add any other details you think would make this first-rate fun for you and your family.

Lord, help our hearts glimpse the heavenly reunion you've planned for us someday.

53

Count the Number of Animals You See in a Day

We encounter a veritable menagerie of beasts during a normal day, only we've become so accustomed to it that we sometimes miss out on the joy of seeing God's creatures at work and play in our world. See how many squirrels, sparrows, dogs, cats, pigeons, lizards, frogs, turtles, and such you can spot during the course of a normal day. The next day, see if you can spot at least one more!

God, our Protector, thanks for never losing sight of me!

54

Skip Stones on a Lake

Contrary to popular opinion, this takes real skill! Take your family to a nearby body of water, stockpile the flattest, roundest stones you can find, then set your pitching arms in motion. See who can skip a rock the farthest, with the most bounces, and with the greatest flair!

Father, make our family like a stone that skips, not like one that sinks.

55

Play Miniature Golf—Blindfolded!

Bring along a blindfold to the miniature golf course, and throw the scorecards out for this one! At each hole, have a different family member don the blindfold and try a hand at sightless putting. Let other family members offer coaching advice to the blindfolded golfer, and be sure to lead that person around the hole so he or she doesn't crash into anything! Afterward, hold a family discussion to determine exactly who had the greatest shot of the day.

Lord Jesus, help us to walk by faith and not by sight through each day of our lives.

56
Listen

Don't just stop to smell the roses—listen to them as well. Take a few minutes today to go on a "listening tour" of your world. Stop right now. What do you hear? Laughter of your children? A bird singing? The refrigerator running? Weeping? Music? Every sound that touches your ears is a miracle. Take time for a miracle today.

Help me hear you today, Jesus.

57
Impersonate Elvis

You may have to educate your children on who Elvis was and why people impersonate him, but once you've got that out of the way, grab a broom (for the stand-up microphone), spin "Jailhouse Rock" or "Heartbreak Hotel" on the CD player, and transform yourselves into the First Family of Elvises (sideburns and sequins optional!). (Warning: Do NOT videotape this event, unless you want decades of ribbing from friends who accidentally view the tape!)

Lord, may our house become a true "Graceland"—a place where your grace reigns supreme.

58
Laugh for No Reason

After all, you don't want to forget how! Practice chuckles, snorts, giggles, guffaws, belly laughs, chortles, snickers, sniggers, titters, tee-hees, cackles, roars, and Santa-style ho-ho-hos. For extra entertainment, try to make your friends laugh for no reason, too. (Laughing is contagious, you know!)

Jesus use me to bring a smile to your face today.

59
Draw a Self-Portrait

Make it a big one, too! Spread a large sheet of paper on the table or the floor (white shelf paper works great for this), spill out all your favorite markers or crayons (or both), set a mirror nearby and get to work recreating your face for the canvas. (If you're particularly artistic, draw portraits of your parents, too.)

God, I praise you for making me in your image.

60
Rate the Best Milk Shakes in Your Community

Make a list of all the fast-food milk-shake makers in your community, then one by one visit each establishment and try their wares. Rate each milk shake on a scale of one to 10 (with 10 being "perfect"). Be sure to take into account things like fluidity, overall flavor, variety of choices, serving size, and so on. (Note: Testing may require more than one sample from each entry!)

Thank you, God, for all the people who help bring us our food.

61
Make a Soap Sculpture

Sure, it looks like just another bar of soap. But deep inside is a boat (or car or dog or whale or hot dog in a bun or caricature of your favorite teacher) waiting to get out! Picture what you want to sculpt, then use a pocket knife to carve away anything that doesn't look like it. (Warning: Great art is almost never appreciated during an artist's lifetime—especially by the artist's family members!)

Jesus, make my life a sculpture of your love in action.

62
Practice Karaoke with the Radio

Use a hairbrush for the microphone. Need we say more?

God, thank you for the gift of music—all kinds of song.

63
List 50 Adjective that Describe God

Sounds tough at first . . . but wait until you get started. You'll be surprised at how much your family knows about God. Brainstorm all the descriptions of God you can, and list them on a sheet of paper. Need help getting started? Try these on your list: "Loving, Creative, All-Knowing, Kind . . . " Afterward, imagine what words God would use to describe each of you.

Help us to always remember all you are to all of us.

64
Ask Questions about the Bible

Read an entire book of the Bible with a notepad right beside you. Each time a question about what you're reading pops into your head, jot it down. (For example, "What exactly is a Leviathan?" "Why should we fear God?" "What does this verse really mean?" and so on.) When you're finished, check Bible commentaries, ask leaders at your church, and get insights from friends to find answers to the questions you wrote.

Holy Spirit, please help me understand your Word.

65
Conduct a "Meaningful Scripture" Survey

Ask ten people this question: "What's one Bible verse that's been meaningful to you in the past, and why was it meaningful?"

You'll be amazed at the wide variety of stories you'll get in response. When you're done, ask yourself the question.

Lord Jesus, let me see your Word at work in my life today.

66
Write Five Unusual Facts about You

Hey, this one's practical, too. Your notes may come in handy if you ever get famous and get asked in an interview, "What's something unusual about you?" (Of course, you might also need this at just about any new small group meeting at your church.) Share your facts with your family members. You never know, you just might discover something new about them too!

God, help me discover something new about you this week.

67
Redesign Your Bedroom

Imagine the sky's the limit. If you could decorate your bedroom without any concern for the cost, what would you do? Paint stars on your ceiling? Wallpaper with silver dollars? Put in triple-decker bunk beds? Have all family members go from room to room and give their best "interior design" ideas. Who knows, there may be one idea you can actually use!

Father, design our family in ways that will reflect you.

68
Eat Dinner without Utensils

Don't act so disgusted! They used to do this all the time during the Middle Ages. So go on and serve up that soup with no spoons (slurping allowed), tear the meat with your bare hands, use your fingers for salad forks, and smear butter with your hands. Once you get past the mess, you'll actually enjoy it (we hope)!

Afterward, ask everyone: Besides eating utensils, what are other things we take for granted in our modern world? (How about light bulbs, microwave ovens, TV sets, cars, and computers for a start?)

Lord, create a hunger in our souls for a taste of your love each day.

69
Face-Paint

Check a local store for a set of face paints, then take them home and let the artistic impulse take over. Look in a mirror to paint your own face, or (if you're trusting souls) let kids paint the parents' faces, and vice versa! If you all turn out particularly well, go out for ice cream to celebrate. (If your results are less than display-worthy, simply take a picture and eat ice cream at home!)

Jesus, when our family is on display, help others to see a picture of you in our faces.

70
Pray for Each Person You Meet in a Day

You can do this two ways: 1) Make a list of names of people you meet as you go through the day, then pray for everyone before you go to bed; or 2) Say a quick prayer for each person as you talk to him or her during the day. Take time to consider what specific needs they might have, and ask God to use you (if possible) to meet those needs.

Lord, teach me to pray.

71
Teach a Bible Study

Few things challenge your creativity more than teaching others, so take the challenge! See if there are any openings to teach a class at your church, volunteer with the youth group, or offer to start an all-new class or home study. You could also lead a short lunchtime study at work. Make use of the wealth of creative teaching resources at your local Christian bookstore to shape your lessons. Afterward, ask yourself: What's one thing I learned through this whole experience?

Spirit of Life, bring the Bible to life for me today.

72
Buy Something Sight-Unseen

$ $ $

Gather the family around the classified ads section of your newspaper, set a price limit for what you'll spend, then pore over the classifieds to find just the right item that sounds too good to be true. Maybe you'll spot a puppy, a Ping-Pong table, or even a new bicycle. Decide on an item, then call the seller and tell them you'll take it—sight unseen. Next, pile everyone in the car and go discover what it is you've really purchased. (Be ready for a surprise, but don't back out of the sale, no matter what.)

God, help us each to find something to like about whatever we purchase!

73
Spill Milk

There's no use crying over spilled milk—especially when you spill it on purpose! Clear out a clean spot on the kitchen floor and carefully pour $1/4$ cup of milk there. (Tell your Mom it's just a new kind of psychological testing!) Let the milk settle, then see what the shape it forms looks like. Is it a sheep? a snowman? your aunt Ruthie? Look at it from a different angle. Does the "picture" change? When you're all done, wipe up with a sponge and pour yourself a fresh glass of chocolate milk for a treat.

Jesus, help me see you at work in my life today.

Create a New Milk Shake (or Two!)

A blender and a gallon of ice cream are wonderful things. Take advantage of these simple pleasures by using them to create never-heard-of-in-the-world milk shakes for your family. Let each family member select ingredients they think will taste best in a milk shake, then blend away! (Some of our favorites are Snickers™-n-banana and chocolate-strawberry-n-pecans.)

Father, thank you for our food, and remind us to share it with others.

Decorate Cupcakes

You thought milk shakes were fun? Wait till you try your hand at cupcakes! Zip over to the grocery store for some canned icing and decorative extras like licorice bits, cake sprinkles, Red Hots™, M&M's™, gumballs, and anything else that looks like fun in the cake or candy aisle. Bring it all home, whip up a batch of cupcakes, then use your supplies to make Da Vinci look like an amateur! Decorate your cupcakes to look like faces, swimming pools, football fields, whatever strikes your fancy. (And remember, if a decoration doesn't turn out quite right, you can always eat it!)

God, thank you for providing all kinds of sweet treats in our lives.

Have a Disney Movie Marathon of Family Favorites

Hit the Disney aisle of the video store some Saturday morning and let each family member choose his or her favorite. (Don't forget non-animated crack-ups like *The Absent-Minded Professor* or *The Love Bug*.) Bring them all home, order pizza, pop some popcorn, and watch them all one after another to create your own Disney extravaganza!

Lord, give us a bit of the imagination that Walt Disney had.

77
Have a Family Slumber Party

Everybody needs an excuse to stay up all night, so why not use a family slumber party? Plan the evening just as if you would if one of your kids had an overnighter with friends. How about midnight bowling? or a family game of "Truth or Dare" (you'll be surprised)? or an all-night Monopoly or Risk tournament? Make sure you've got plenty of junk food, games to play, fun music for the stereo, and a room full of sleeping bags for when you all finally tire out (say, around 5:00 A.M.).

Thank you, Father, for never pausing to sleep, for watching over our family at all hours of the day and night.

78
Guess the Weight of 10 Things in Your Home

No people included in weight-guessing on this one! But aren't you curious exactly how much a bottle of Dr. Pepper™ weighs? Or that lamp in the living room? Or all your schoolbooks? Or laundry basket full of tennis shoes? Now's your chance to find out. Make a list of any 10 things that will fit on a bathroom scale, then take turns guessing how much each one weighs. After all guesses are made, set your items on the scale. Award a standing ovation to the person who guesses the closest to an item's actual weight.

Lord, help our family to shed a few pounds if we need to.

79
Watch People at the Mall

Hang out at a nearby mall for an hour or so, and check out all who pass by. Sit on a bench and make up stories about the people you see. Maybe the guy in the sunglasses thinks he's Tom Cruise. Perhaps the two girls giggling down the walkway are practicing for a laugh-track audition. It's possible the couple holding hands in front of the jewelry store just got engaged (wonder how he proposed?). And maybe the guy eating a hot dog in the food court is really just watching you!

Jesus, help me to see all people as you see them.

80
Measure Your Height in Bottle Caps

Or popsicle sticks. (You might need to eat a few popsicles and drink a few sodas to get the proper supplies for this one. Tell your parents we said it was OK and that it won't spoil your dinner.)

Regardless of what other people may think of me, Jesus, help me always to stand tall in your eyes.

81
Try a New Pair of Sunglasses

Drugstores are great for finding really unusual sunglasses. Grab a friend, head out to one nearby, and spend a few minutes trying on sunglasses. Be sure you're near a mirror. Which ones make you look eccentric? Like a movie star? What hairstyles should go with particular pairs of shades? Afterward, ask yourself: What about me never changes, no matter how I look on the outside?

Lord, give me a clear spiritual vision that allows me to see you at all times.

82
Read *Peter Pan* by J. M. Barrie

Flying children, lost boys, mermaids, pirates, and houses under-ground—*Peter Pan* has it all! Spend a half hour each night reading aloud this delightfully imaginative book for the whole family. Let older children take turns reading aloud as well. As the story progresses, invite family members to draw pictures illustrating how they imagine the people and places look in the story. (And remember, you never really have to grow up either!)

Mike and Amy Nappa

If every one of us becomes like a lost boy, please come find us quickly, Lord Jesus.

83
Prepare a Celebrity Interview

Wouldn't it be fun if your family members were reporters for *People* magazine, and your first assignment was to interview your favorite celebrities? (Hey, it could happen!) What would you ask those people? What would you really like to find out about Rosie O'Donnell or Amy Grant or Denzel Washington or Chuck Swindoll or Morgan Freeman or Whitney Houston? Pretend you're going to do those interviews, and write out your questions. (For extra fun, pretend you're the celebrities. What would a reporter ask you?)

Father, please help us choose wisely the people we choose to imitate.

84
Plan Your Dream Vacation

If your family could spend a week anywhere, doing anything at all, what would you do? Would you go to Narnia? Visit NASA headquarters? Scuba dive in the Hawaiian islands? The sky's the limit on this one (literally), so gather the household and start dreaming!

God, plant in us the dreams you have for our family to fulfill.

85
Compliment Everyone You Meet in a Day

See if you can get beyond "You look nice today" or "Gee, your perfume smells good." Look for unique, sincere compliments you can pay to everyone you cross paths with today. Tell the coffee shop clerk you appreciate her excellent customer service. Thank your coworker for being a great encourager. Tell your teenager you admire her commitment to pray. Remind your preschooler he's got great imagination. And (of course) tell your spouse he or she has great taste when it comes to the opposite sex!

God, you are awesome!

86
Think of a Reason for Celebrating Each Day in a Week

Is it Charlie Brown's birthday? National Hug Your Dog Day? The anniversary of the first time you watched Monday Night Football? The Day You Finished Your Homework? The First Sighting of the Bottom of the Laundry Basket? There's a reason to rejoice each day, so choose the best reasons for your family to party this week—even if it's just because we live in a world where Nerf™ toys exist!

Thank you, Jesus, for being our ultimate reason to celebrate!

87
Pray with a Phone Receiver in Your Hand

Make that cosmic connection with a physical prop to help. Of course, you don't need a phone to talk to God, but sometimes the picture of speaking to God over a telephone wire can help you focus your conversations. Imagine Jesus called to chat and you answered the phone. What would you talk about? What will he tell you? As you say "amen" and hang up the phone, ask God to help you hear when God calls again.

Lord, please never let us get "disconnected" in prayer.

See How Many Uses There Are for a Frisbee™

An orphanage in South America once mistook a shipment of donated Frisbees for dishes. They used them for weeks as plates until some kids discovered they could fly. So what else could you and your family use Frisbees for? Grab a few flying disks and start experimenting!

God, grant us the ability to think out of the box sometimes.

89

Listen to *Adventures in Odyssey* on the Radio

The beauty of radio drama is that it requires imagination to go along with the dialogue and sound effects. *Focus on the Family* has raised radio drama to an art form with its audio series, *Adventures in Odyssey*. Call your local Christian radio station for show times in your area, or stop by a Christian bookstore and purchase a few cassettes or CDs. Then gather as a family and listen with your imaginations "on" to picture the scenes acted out on your stereo speakers. Decide what the characters might look like, puzzle out how they created the accompanying sounds, and try to figure out how the story will end. (Beware of cliffhangers, though!)

Thank you, Father, for the gift of imagination.

90

Play "Football Announcer"

Next time there's a good football game on turn the sound on the TV all the way down, then have family members take turns trying to "call the action" as if you were a famous announcer working the game. See if you can keep up with the plays, sort out the penalties, and (of course) do your best imitations of John Madden.

In our lives, Lord, help us to trust you to lead us to victory!

91

Live One Day without Electricity

OK, you can leave the refrigerator on, but turn other appliances off! That means no electric lights, no TV, no fans, no blow-dryers, no curling irons, no electric ovens, no coffee makers, and so on. Pretend you live in the old West, or have to make do during a freak storm that knocks the power out at your home. See how creative you can be in adjusting to life without the advantage of electricity. You just might surprise yourself!

Show us, Jesus, what we really need to live in your will—and what we need to do without.

92

Fast

Try doing without food for a day. See what you can substitute to take your mind of food. Some like to pray when they feel hungry; others like to read the Bible; still others take a nap. Do whatever works best for you. Afterward, ask yourself: Why does my body crave food so much? How does not feeding it affect my body? What can I learn from this experience that is true of spiritual nourishment as well?

God, help my mind, body, and spirit bring you into a sharper focus today.

93

Be a Secret Pal

Make it your goal to secretly encourage another family member for a month. Draw names out of a hat to decide who will be a secret pal for whom. Then spend the next 30 days looking for creative ways to brighten each other's days. (Older family members may want to assist younger ones in this.) Leave notes in sock drawers, stealthily deposit small presents on each other's pillows, write

Mike and Amy Nappa

a compliment in shaving cream on the bathroom mirror, and more. Have a secret pal appreciation party at the end of the month to reveal your true identities.

Jesus, thanks for being our eternal friend.

94
Call a Phone Booth, Just to Find Out Who'll Answer

Next time you go out for pizza or to the mall, jot down the phone numbers of the pay phones nearby. Later, when you and you're friends can't think of anything to do, give the pay phones a ring. See how much you can discover about the responsible soul who answers.

Jesus, please make just the right person answer!

95
Visit a Zoo

God's creativity is remarkably seen in creation, so spend a day to take a look at it! Count the colors on the tropical birds, or make a list of the most unique talents in the zoo (such as a bat's ability to fly in the dark), find the beast most likely to be mistaken for Ted Koppel, and mostly just take in the vast creativity God used when making the world. Afterward, ask family members: How was God creative when he made me?

Awesome Creator, thank you for making me just the way you did.

96

Learn a Song on the Harmonica

You can do this the official way (buy a book an teach yourself the proper technique and notes to play) or the unofficial, Nappaland way, grab a harmonica and start experimenting. Either way, expect a few misses before you learn your harmonica hit! Make it a goal for each family member to be able to blow out at least one song by the end of a month's time. If you're good, take the show on the road (or at least to a friend's house for dinner).

Loving Spirit, help us hear your melodies of love in our lives.

97

Use Chopsticks

For starters, eat a meal with them. Once you've got that down, move on to the "hard stuff," like inventing drum solos on the table with them, building log cabins, pinning up your hair, twirling them like batons, and dropping them in a bottle. You get the idea.

Show us, Lord, a little bit of you in every culture we may encounter in our lives.

98

Create a Work of Art out of K'Nex™

Trust us, it can be done. Our local museum gave K'Nex™ to a number of artists that live in our area, and they filled an entire exhibit room with K'Nex art! You can set your sights a little lower, though. How about filling your dining-room table with K'Nex™art? See if you can make an island floating in a blue lagoon, or a sculpture of a hot fudge sundae, or even a toupee for dear old Dad! In case you're not familiar with K'Nex, it's a kids' interlocking construction set similar to Legos™. K'Nex are available at most discount stores and also at toy stores.

Please see the art in me, dear Jesus.

99
Restyle Your Hair

Admit it. You were getting kind of tired of it anyway. Now here we are giving you an excuse to do something you already wanted to do—change the way your hair looks. Mousse it straight up, add blond streaks, get a perm, comb it all back, comb it all forward, try a ponytail (or two or three), add a few beads, and generally play around with all kinds of new combinations. One warning though: It takes a long time to make up for a bad haircut, so think twice before you decide to chop it all off!

Never let me forget, Jesus, that you are always in style.

100
Buy the Most Unusual Thing at a Thrift Store

One person's hand-me-outs could be your family's treasure! Take a trip to a nearby thrift store and look for the most unusual item you can find there. Some of the best stuff to look for are 1970s-style furniture, T-shirts with wacky sayings on them, knickknacks for your mantelpieces, and so on. (One person we know scored a 1960s era album of Don Ho singing gospel.) Have family members vote on what they think is the most unusual—then buy it! Take it home as a reminder of your relentless pursuit of the unusual.

As a family, Lord, we ask that you'd help us appreciate and enjoy the treasures hidden within each of us.

101
Have a Family "Show and Tell"

Who says first graders are the only ones to have this kind of fun? Plan a family "Show and Tell" every once in a while. Pick a variety of themes such as "My Favorite Bugs," "My Best Christmas Present Ever," and "My Favorite Pastimes." Invite each family member to bring something, and take turns showing and telling in your living room. (For extra fun, have show and tell when relatives visit.)

Jesus, thank you for "showing" your love by dying on the cross, and giving us opportunities to "tell" others how you were raised from the dead.

102

Buy a Stuffed Animal that Looks Like You

Search the aisles for that one plush animal that could be your twin—and buy it (with a little help from Mom and Dad, of course). Are you cute and cuddly? Then a teddy bear would be just for you. Known for your crooked grin? Then it's a stuffed crocodile for you. Have bright orange stripes and a springy tail? Then bring home Tigger from *Winnie the Pooh*. (And remember, the search is half the fun of this spark idea!)

God, help me always remember that in all the world I'm the only me you've made.

103

Draw on the Driveway or Sidewalk

A bucket of chalk and a freshly washed driveway can go a long, long way. Gather the family outside, spill the chalk all over, and spend an hour or so making a mural on the driveway or sidewalk. Let family members each fill up a section of the drive, or have everyone join in one big picture. And remember it's OK to have things like a blue iguana, a crooked house, and stick-figure parents standing around!

Father, help us always remember that our family frames the pictures of our individual lives.

104

Rent a Tandem Bicycle

As the song proclaims, you will look sweet on a bicycle built for two! Choose a partner and rent a tandem bicycle for a few hours. Ride around your community, checking out the sights. Challenge a skateboarder to a race. Sing "Bicycle Built for Two" at all stop lights. Take turns pedaling in the front seat. While in the back seat, see how long you can fool your mate by only pretending to pedal. And generally have an old-fashioned day of fun!

Lord, be my leading partner today and every day.

105
Build a Snow Turtle

Thinking about building a snowman next time it snows? Everybody's done that. But how many people can boast that they've built a snow turtle? Or a snow alligator? Or a snow cadillac? Or a snow-turtle-watching-a-snow-Cadillac-being-chased-by-a-snow-alligator-through-a-snow-swamp? Well, you can if you'll put this book down long enough to enjoy a snowy day with your family! Go ahead and have fun. We'll be here when you come back in for a warm blanket and some hot cocoa.

Heavenly Father, thanks for giving us memories to last a lifetime—even on snowy days!

106
Do a Science Experiment

Check out a book of science experiments from your local library Enlist your parent's help in trying some of the creative experiments in there. For example, did you know there are experiments that show how to use scientific principles to put a straw through a potato with your bare hands? Or suck a whole egg into a bud vase unharmed? (While you're experimenting, see if you can find a scientific principle to explain why socks disappear in the dryer!)

God, help me see you today through the science of your creation.

107
Play H-O-R-S-E with a Paper Wad and a Trash Can

You don't need a gymnasium to have fun with this age-old game as long as you've got a crumpled paper (for the ball), a trash can (for the basket), and your living room (for the court). Play the same rules as in basketball (one letter for each missed shot; whoever accumulates all the letters loses). Of course you'll have to throw out all dribbling rules, but you can add other unique elements such as a requirement to sit during all shots, to flick instead of throw the paper wads, and to make sure the loser does the dishes!

Father, thanks for the inexpensive fun our family can enjoy!

108
Buy a CD by Someone You've Never Heard of

Look through the selection of a used-CD store for just the right album—the one you never knew existed! Check out categories you don't normally listen to (such as classical or oldies), look for the CD cover that looks most interesting, then take a chance on a new artist. Buy the CD, take it home, and listen to it from beginning to end at least once, just to see if the music lives up to the cover. (If it doesn't, give it to Dad for Father's Day. Tell him it's from us.)

Make this a good choice, Lord. (Please.)

109
Go Somewhere You've Never Been

Trust us: You have yet to experience all the unique "atmosphere" this world offers. Think of all the everyday places you've never been, then plan to go there. For example, you might visit a comic-book store, a pawn shop, a high-school track meet, an ethnic grocery store, a nearby cave, a rock concert, a prison, or even the Grand Canyon! Afterward, ask yourself: What was one unique thing I noticed about this place? Why did I wait so long to visit here? What does that tell me about myself?

Expand my horizons, Lord Jesus, so that I may see you every-where I go.

110

Make a Video Titled, "Our Average Day"

Have each family member take turns taping video highlights of his or her day, with appropriate commentary. For example, a parent might videotape his or her office, comments from coworkers, and activities from the day; a teenager or child might videotape intro-ductions to his or her teachers, time spent on a homework assign-ment, and lunch in the cafeteria. Put all the videos on one tape, and afterward view the tape as a family to get a glimpse of what you all experience during a normal day.

Jesus, let us all remember that we need you every hour, every day.

111

Make a Recording Titled, "Sound Effects from My Day"

Instead of carrying a video camera, have family members each carry a cassette recorder and turn it on periodically during the day. Capture things like a traffic jam, a staff meeting, part of math class, after-school TV, snatches of a phone conversation, and more. At the end of the day, take turns playing your recordings for the entire family.

Father, teach us to hear your voice each day.

112

Start a Bug Collection

All you need is a jar, a lid with holes in it (so bugs can breathe), a twig or two (for picking up bugs you don't want to touch), and a few leaves and a little bit of water for bugs to eat and drink. If you want to go all out, take along a butterfly net to catch flying insects. Then go exploring! Look around your backyard, grandma's house, a park, the playground, wherever a bug might hang out. Try not to catch two of the same kind of insect, and look for ones with unique colors and talents. Afterward, examine your bug collection for awhile, then set everything free and start over again tomorrow.

God, help me find the most interesting bug I can today.

113
Name All the Puppies in the Window

Gather outside a pet store, and instead of asking, "How much is that puppy in the window?" ask, "If I were naming that puppy, what would I call it?" Does the blue heeler look like an "Elvis"? The poodle like a "Snootums"? Does the really cute, dark-furred one with the irresistible personality rate the grand name, "Mike"? (Or is that for the mousy-looking one drooling in the corner?) For extra fun, give the pet-store employees dog names, too. (But don't tell them we said to do that!)

Heavenly Father, the best name you ever gave us was when you called us your children. Thanks for that.

114
Play Photographer for a Day

Arm yourselves with cameras and embark on a search for the world's best photographic scenes. Pretend you are on assignment for *Life* magazine. Visit a park and capture a couple holding hands. Look for sunlight streaming through trees. Get a zoom-lens close-up of a squirrel eating a nut. Have each family member find at least a dozen stunning visual images and capture those images on film.

Help us notice something we wouldn't normally see today, Lord.

115

Plan the Perfect Date (No Dollar Limit!)

You'll never know if you've been on the perfect date unless you know what to expect, so start planning now! Imagine you have no financial limits . . . What will you do? Take a helicopter ride over the Empire State Building? Jet to Maui for dinner? Go para-sailing in the Caribbean? The sky's the limit, so take off!

At least once in my life, God, grant that I might experience a dream date like the one I came up with.

116

Plan the Perfect Date for $5 or Less

For those of us who are, shall we say, financially challenged, what we can't buy with money we have to make up for in imagination. But no worry, although imagination is free, it's not cheap, and our escorts value it highly. Pick your brain for imaginative dates under $5 such as star-watching, taking in the Dancing Waters show at the Disneyland Hotel, touring the local garage sales, flying a kite, and whatever else your fertile mind can dream up. Choose your top three ideas, and try them out on a double date with your parents and/or teen children.

Jesus, help me enjoy this life no matter what my bank account looks like!

117

Unpack the Groceries According to Color

Next time you bring home the groceries, unpack everything according to its color. For example, unload all the red items first (apples, Coca-Cola™, and the like), then the green items next (pickles, lettuce, 7-Up™, and such), and so on. Take turns choosing which colors to unpack, and be sure to check all the way down to the bottom of each bag before starting on a new color!

Father, thanks for providing the nourishment we need each day—and for including chocolate once in a while, too!

118
Bowl with Your Nondominant Hand

Yes, you'll look silly. Yes, your family members will laugh at you. Yes, strangers will think you're a bit clumsy. But this simple, silly change will cause you to creatively adjust everything you know (or don't know!) about bowling. Be sure to play at least one "Left Hand against Right Hand" game in which you bowl for two players, "Mr. Left" and "Mr. Right." See if you can predict within five pins what the final scores will be.

Lord, make your strength perfect in our weaknesses.

119
Transform Your Home into a Cruise Ship

For one day, imagine your home has been miraculously changed into a cruise ship! Decide which side of the house is starboard and which is port. Open your portholes (windows) and shout "bon voyage!" to the neighbors. Appoint a "cruise director" to plan activities. Visit the galley and eat at the "captain's table." Go "on deck" (outside) for swimming (use an inflatable kiddie pool). Dress up for a grand ball (dance to the stereo in the living room). Finish the day by retiring to your "staterooms" to sleep. (Don't forget mints on the pillows.)

Father, help us steer our "cruise ship" of life directly toward your kingdom each day.

120
Go Climb a Tree

Find a sturdy trunk and see if you can get all family members in the tree at once. While in the tree, take time to notice your change of perspective. What looks different from up there? What interesting things do you see in the branches? Think together to design the most extravagant tree house possible in that tree.

Jesus, let us see our world through your eyes today.

Make a "Map of the Stars' Homes"

Of course, you and your friends are the stars! Photocopy the map in the phone book (for your own personal use), then find and mark with stick-on stars the locations where you and your 10 favorite friends and relatives live. Number each star and make a corresponding "brochure" that tells who lives in that spot and something special about them (such as, "Home of Christopher Nappa, star who once owned a dog that could climb a tree.")

Jesus, make me your biggest fan!

Race a Frog

Visit a local pet center and let each family member purchase the frog he or she thinks will be the fastest and farthest jumper. Also pick up a few frog-food treats (ask the clerk for suggestions). Then take everything home, use cardboard to set up a racing trough, put the food at one end and the frogs at the other and shout, "Go!" See which person's frog makes it to the food first. Run as many races as you like. Afterward, have someone read aloud Mark Twain's classic story "The Jumping Frog of Calaveras County" for the family.

God, as we race through life, remind us to stop and rest on the "lily pads" we find along the way.

Visit a Foreign Country—Without Leaving Home

Designate a night for the visit, then since you can't actually go to Poland (or England or Egypt or Mexico or wherever), bring that country to you. See if you can get a travel poster from travel agent. Have each family member discover one interesting fact about your chosen country (check the library) and be prepared to share it with everyone. Prepare food that's common in the country. See if you can find a CD or tape from that place. Learn a game from your chosen country and play it. Afterward, brainstorm what people in Poland might do if they "visited" the United States in their homes as well.

Lord, give us a heart to share your love with people from other countries.

124

Paraphrase

Pick your favorite chapter of the Bible (1 Corinthians 13? John 3? Psalm 23? Romans 10?). Then begin with the first verse and rewrite the whole chapter in your own words, explaining what you read in terms that are easy for you to understand. (Warning: Kenneth Taylor once did this, and got so hooked he paraphrased the whole Bible! It eventually was published as *The Living Bible.*)

Make your Word a treasure in my life this week.

125

Sing in the Rain

It really is as much fun as it seems in the classic movie—even if you can't dance like Gene Kelly! Next time it's really pouring outside, take any adventurous family members outside for a little splashin'-n-singin' time in the rain. (Umbrellas optional for this one!)

(Note: Our trusty editor, who himself is a veteran of many rains, wisely points out that being struck by lightning "ain't fun." Although we're afraid to ask how he knows this, we must agree he's probably right. So, please be cautious before going outside for this activity. If lightning and thunder are nearby, wait for a gentler shower before exercising your vocal chords in the rain!)

Thank you, Creator God, for refreshing rain, and for the rainbows that sometimes accompany the rain as well.

126
Host a Garage Sale

Get your family's entrepreneurial juices flowing with this creative spark idea and you could actually earn back the price you paid for this book! Have everyone contribute something to the sale, then work together to festively display all your items as if you were managing an upscale department store. Add a table with refreshments for sale, then let the bargains begin! During the day, encourage wheeling and dealing, take a few trades in place of cash, and spend part of your profits on pizza afterward.

Thanks for investing your love in us, Jesus.

127
Mow a Heart Shape in Your Lawn

Tell a family member it's simply a reminder that you love him or her "mow" each day!

Spirit of Love, put your love into our hearts.

128
Play Hopscotch

Contrary to popular opinion, it takes real talent to play hopscotch. You must be able to count to 10 accurately, hop your way through a dizzying array of possibilities, and pitch a rock with the same skill as a major league pitcher. But even if you aren't perfect at all these things, you still can admire that anonymous gamer who invented an entertaining activity using only rocks and sidewalk. So, grab a few rocks, mark out the playing field, and lead your family in a rousing tribute game for the creative soul who invented hopscotch!

From skinned knees and bruised egos, please protect us, Lord.

Mix Up the Board Games

If you're like us, most of your board game pieces are already mixed up anyway—so take advantage of that! Pull out three or four of your family's favorite games, take a few pieces from each, and create an all-new game that combines elements of all the others. Perhaps instead of going to jail in Monopoly™, a player is banished to Candyland™ and must stay there until he or she passes Mr. Mint. Or maybe you must roll a Yahtzee™ before you can get married in the game of Life. Ready? Let the games begin!

Thank you, Holy Father, for the power to make something good come out of the mixed up things in life!

Copy a Work of Art

Take the family to a nearby art museum, arm each person with a sketch pad and pencil, then set out to copy your favorite works of art. (Tell everyone that stick figures are OK.) Let each family member select at least one work of art that everyone must copy. Afterward compare your drawings and decide which of you is most likely to become a starving artist!

Jesus, each day we live on this earth, show us how to "copy" the work of art that is you.

Sculpt Foil

You thought Play-Doh™ was fun? Wait until you see what you can do with a roll of tinfoil and a little imagination. Gather around the dinner table and give each person several squares of aluminum foil. Then have everyone create the following sculptures: Something from nature; something in our house; something to play with; something from your imagination.

Remind us today, Lord, that you are the Potter, and we are your clay.

Make a Gingerbread Neighborhood

Aaaaah, an excuse to be creative and eat candy at the same time! Is life great or what? Don't wait until Christmas to do this creative idea. Try it anytime. Make gingerbread cookies in various shapes (or substitute graham crackers), buy gobs of decorative candies, use frosting for "glue," and begin construction. Have everyone design his or her own house. Then set them all in a row to make your family's own little gingerbread neighborhood.

Let us lean on you, Father, as we build our family on your Word.

133

Learn to Say "I Love You" in Several Languages

Give each family member the responsibility for learning how to say "I love you" in two foreign languages. (Check the library, ask teachers and friends, call a local college for help, check a CD-ROM, etc.) Then teach each other what you've learned until you're all fluent in the language of love. (Be sure to practice by saying your phrases to each other often.)

Padre, te amamos!

134

Learn a Song in Sign Language

Ask your church's song leader or the choir teacher at your school for help. You can also check out books on sign language from the library that tell how to sign different words. When you're ready, select a simple song, learn how to sign all the words, then perform it for your family, singing along as you sign. Afterward, ask yourself: What would it be like for me if I couldn't hear music?

Lord, even when I don't speak a word, let others know by the way I live that I'm your child.

Go Window-Shopping for Cinderella's Grand Ball

OK, we admit it. This idea is mostly for the women in your family. (Guys, just assume you'll wear a tuxedo, OK?) Ladies, imagine you've been invited to Cinderella's grand ball and you've just got nothing to wear! So jump in your pumpkin coach and visit the malls and boutiques in search of the most extravagant, elegant, refined, exquisite, ornate gown to impress the prince and the rest of the royal family. (Be sure to be home by midnight!)

Father, never let me forget that I'm already royalty in your sight.

Design a Car that Truly Fits Your Lifestyle

Perhaps you can't own the car of your dreams, but at least you can design it! Forget about all those fancy-schmancy perks like leather seats and wiper blades on headlights. Instead, create a car that will truly fit your lifestyle. For example, if you have many pets, why not a van with self-vacuuming "pet seats" (complete with seatbelts) in the back? Or for the chocoholics in the family, how about a cool, dry chocolate bin beside each chair? Or a robot arm that automatically puts on your makeup while you're driving—and allows you to keep your eyes on the road. You get the idea. When you're done, take a quick dash out to your car and see if you can safely modify it to bring at least one of your ideas to life!

Redesign my life into your image, Lord Jesus!

137
Look through Model Homes

Now that you've designed your dream cars, scope out your dream houses as well. Look for nearby new housing developments and take the family for a walk through all the model homes. Have family members decide which rooms would be theirs, which of the model home decorations they'd like to keep, and what they'd like best and least about each house. Afterward, tour your own home as if it were one last model home to visit.

Heavenly Father, please make our home a place where you are always present.

138
Teach an Old Dog a New Trick

They say you can't teach an old dog new tricks, but here's your chance to prove them wrong! See if you can help your dog catch up on something it may have missed out on as a puppy. Perhaps it never learned how to sit, or catch a flying disk, or fetch, or play dead, or whatever. See what kind of rewards and practice it takes to teach your dog one or more of these tricks. (Note: If you really can't teach your old dog a new trick, just tell your family you've taught the dog not to give in to peer pressure!)

No matter how old I get, Lord, help me always to be ready to learn something new from you.

139
Try a New Recipe

Drop a finger at random in a cookbook or cooking magazine and try out that recipe no matter what—even if it's braised beets and herring! (If you want to give yourself a few options, select three recipes at random and choose the one that seems most palatable.) See if you can discover a new treat that's good enough to share with your family.

Give me a spirit of adventure today, Jesus!

140
Eat Your Veggies (and Fruit)

Survey the produce aisle at your local grocery store for the most unusual produce item you see. (Did you know there's such a thing as carambola?) Let each family member choose one piece of produce your family has never had before, and take it all home. If necessary, prepare the food according to the appropriate specifications and serve it up for dinner. Afterward, work as a group to rate the new vegetables and fruits on a scale of 1 to 10, with 1 being "not fit for human consumption" and 10 being "almost as good as chocolate!"

Thank you, dear Creator, for making such a wide variety of food!

141
Invent a New Pizza Topping

Stopped in at Planet Hollywood once only to discover the special of the day was this: Cap'n Crunch™ pizza. What was there to do? Had to try it. It had grilled chicken rolled in Cap'n Crunch crumbs, and was terrific! Which makes us certain there are other un-thought-of pizza combinations lurking in your minds—so let them loose! Buy some premade pizza dough, slap on spaghetti sauce, cheese, and your imagination. How about peach pizza? or peas and corn? Try anything your family is game for, and if it turns out to be great, send the recipe to Planet Hollywood. Maybe your combination will be the special of the day sometime!

Remind us daily, Jesus, that you plus us is always a winning combination!

142

Take a Walk in a Cemetery

A cemetery holds more than just coffins, it keeps a thousand stories on its grounds. Take your family to a nearby cemetery and see if you can discover some of the stories it holds. Read the grave markers. Find the funniest epitaph, the person who lived the longest, the most moving spot, the prettiest flowers, and so on. Imagine what a deceased person's life might have been like, and discuss what you'd like written on your grave stone. Afterward, pause to thank God for the stories each person's life leaves behind—including your own.

Jesus, please be the main character in the stories our lives tell.

143

Capture a Sunrise

Take time to witness the silent explosion of colors that accompanies the start of each day. Ask yourself why God chose to announce mornings in such a creatively kaleidoscopic way, and why it's so easy to take these daily fireworks for granted. Before you leave, think of one way you can reflect a sunrise in your family's life today.

Heavenly Father, let me shine your light in the life of my family today.

144

Go on a Junkyard Treasure Hunt

One man's trash is another man's treasure, so go find that gem at your nearest junk collector's location. Make it a goal to find one item that your family would treasure—even if no one else thinks it would be worth a penny! Is it that remarkably lifelike bronze garden statue? Hubcaps that fit a 1957 Chevy? Slightly used fuzzy dice that hang from a rearview mirror? If you can afford to, buy the item and take it home. If it's too expensive, take a picture of it.

Afterward, read Jesus' parables about hidden treasure found in Matthew 13:44-45. Ask yourselves: What pearls in my life are sometimes hidden from my view?

This week, dear God, show us how valuable each person in our family is.

145

Hold a Jellybean Contest

Take a jar filled with jellybeans with you to school (or wherever else you go) today, and invite friends, teachers, and family members alike to guess how many candies are in the jar. Make a few guesses yourself, just for fun. At the end of the day, count the jellybeans and see who was able to guess closest to the correct number (yourself not in included). Tomorrow, award that person the jar refilled with jellybeans as his or her reward.

Help me be a sweet treat for my family and friends today, God!

146

Host a Murder

Of course we're talking about the party game here, not the real thing! Check out your local toys and games shop for this creative line of entertainment. Then decide which characters your guests should play, send out the invitations, and follow the detailed instructions to make this mystery-solving experience a party success. (We think the butler did it!)

Lord Jesus, let me treasure life experience today.

147

Dye Eggs for Any Holiday but Easter

Admit it, you get a kick out of painting eggs all kinds of colors each Easter—and so do we! But it doesn't have to be Easter before you can dye eggs again. Why not dye Christmas eggs and hang them on the tree for a day or two? Or go on an Independence Day egg hunt? (Give a prize to whoever finds the egg with the flag painted on it.) Or even color eggs just to brighten up breakfast on your birthday? After all, you can celebrate Jesus' resurrection each day of the year—not just on Easter Sunday.

Hallelujah! You are risen indeed!

148
Celebrate Christmas in July

As long as we're mixing up holidays, let's celebrate Jesus' birth in swim trunks instead of snowsuits! Hold a Christmas in July party, complete with a tree, lights, mistletoe, football, eggnog, a big dinner, the Christmas story, and (of course) presents. Sometime during the party, have everyone tell their favorite Christmas memories and traditions. Then exchange gifts and sing a few Christmas carols loud enough for the neighbors to hear!

You are the best gift ever, Jesus, and we praise and thank you for that.

149
Slide

See if you can invent three all-new, never-done-before ways to go down a slide. (Take a parent along to make sure nothing you try is potentially harmful.) Everybody's slid in a seated position, and even tried headfirst down a slide. But what else is possible? Sideways? With a puppy on your back? Sitting in a teddy bear's lap? Curled up in a ball? Think of your best (and safe) ideas and try them out! If they're really good, convince Mom or Dad to try them, too.

God, keep my mind creative, my body healthy, and my spirit seeking after you.

150
Build a Sand Castle

You'll need a beach or a sandbox for this one. Have the family work together to create a castle fit for a (sandy) king! Damp sand works best for this, and paper cups make great molds for turrets. Include things like a moat around the castle, a drawbridge (made of sticks or cardboard), use a funnel to make garrets, and more. When you're ready to leave, pretend a band of giants (you) is attacking the castle and reducing it to ruins!

Lord, help us build our family relationships on a firm foundation—your love.

151
Build a Tootsie Roll™ Cabin

Take a big bag of Tootsie Rolls and use the candies as "logs" in a cabin construction. You can make a one-room cabin (one square building), or a whole cabin complex. Set the whole thing on a paper plate foundation and get to work. Cut out spaces for windows (which means you'll have to eat whatever you cut out—so make lots of windows), add a log chimney, and ask your parents when you can build a life-size version of your model!

Lord Jesus, thank you for fun stuff, like Tootsie Rolls and families!

152
Watch a Washing Machine

Sounds odd, we know, but when our son was five he discovered for us the amazing world that goes on inside a washing machine cycle. Get the machine going with the lid open (you'll have to push down the button normally tabbed by the lid), then settle in for a spray of motion and colors as the clothing stains disappear. See if you can visually follow one article of clothing through the cycle. Predict which sock will get lost. Blow on the bubbles the soap creates. If your family decides they want to watch, charge them admission to the show!

Create a clean heart in me, O God.

153

Gaze into a Candle's Flame

Fire is a dangerous but fascinating thing. Keep this idea under control by simply lighting one candle. Then turn off all lights and watch the flickering flame in the dark. How many colors do you see? How much of the room does this tiny flame illuminate? How does the flame change its shape? What's one thing you've never noticed about fire before? (As long as you're satisfying your curiosity with this idea, you might as well eat a candlelight dinner with your spouse as well!)

Set my heart on fire with love for you, Jesus.

154

Create Hand Shadows on the Wall

This works best in a room with a night light, so crowd everyone in there. Next, see what kinds of unusual shapes you can "paint" on the wall with the shadows of your hands. Make the obligatory bunnies and crocodiles to start, then get really busy. See if you can join with another family member to make a two-headed horse, or arrange your fingers on top of a fist to form a king with a crown. Before you're done, make one large, all-hands-involved mural of shadows for the grand finale.

Heavenly Father, cover our family in the shadow of your wings today.

155

Finish this Sentence:
"If I Could Find Anything Under My Bed
Tomorrow Morning, It'd Be . . . "

Just before bedtime, have each family member dream a bit, then share how they'd complete that sentence. Before sleeping, pray that if it's best for you, God would make those dreams come true.

God, let us wake up in the morning to find you at work in our lives.

156

Imagine What Clouds Resemble

It's incredible how much we miss simply because we forget to look up. Next time you have a wonderful, cloudy day, look up in the sky and let your imagination see what's there. Do the clouds form a castle in the air? A bear with its paw extended? Your cousin Lenny's hair? See if others can identify a specific cloud simply by your description of it. (And if you get caught in the rain, see creative spark # 125!)

Lord, thank you for creating beauty in the clouds.

157

Play "What If . . . "

Add pizzazz to a boring road trip with this game. One person starts by making a "What if . . . " statement, such as "What if this car were a rocket ship?" or "What if furniture was made out of chocolate?" Others in the car respond with "Then . . . " statements like, "If this car were a rocket ship, then I'd be driving!" or "If furniture were made of chocolate, I'd want Snickers™ couch!" Play as long as you like, or until you get hungry and stop for dessert.

Lord, help us to live out the answer to the question, "What if our family really made God first in life?"

158

Make a Rainbow out of M&M's™

Tell your Mom you absolutely must have a big bag of M&M's™, otherwise your creative growth will be stunted by your inability to do this idea! Spread the candies all over the dining-room table and separate them by color. Make arched rows of each color, and place them side by side to create your rainbow. When you're done, ask yourself: If there were a pot of gold at the end of this rainbow, what would I do with it?

God, let every color of the rainbow remind me of you.

159

Order Someone Else's Dinner

Have dinner tonight at a fast-food restaurant—but don't order your food. Have each person order another family member's dinner, no prompting allowed from others! Draw names to see who orders for whom. See how well you know each other's likes and dislikes when it comes to food, and be sure to include condiments and drinks for each meal as well.

Jesus, help us serve each other well tonight!

160

Find Something New in Your Car

Look for something you've never noticed before—a new dial on the dash, the color of the bottom of the backseat floor mat, a tear in the upholstery, a message in Japanese, instructions for changing a tire, the place to put in brake fluid, whatever. You'll be amazed at what you discover. (With any luck, you just might find some coins under the seat cushions!)

Show us new ways you're blessing our family this week.

Ponder an Imponderable™

Life if full of unanswered questions, so much so that author David Feldman has made a career out of finding answers to those questions. He's discovered important things like why dogs have wet noses, why we wake up with bad breath, how the football got its shape, and more. Now you can follow in Feldman's footsteps. Discover answers to your own imponderables like "Why does Mom always call me my older siblings' names?" "Why does my baby brother wait until I'm changing his diaper to go to the bathroom?" "Which is better, a big piece of chocolate to share, or a small piece all to myself?" Remember, some imponderables take more research than others!

Lord, help me understand more about you this week.

Make a House of Cards

This is harder than you think! You may have to fold a few cards, put lines in the carpet, and stop breathing whenever you're near it, but it is possible. Work together on one giant house, or make several smaller, individual houses. When you're all done, jump up and down to create a mock "earthquake," and see what best survives the "tremors." Afterward, you can read aloud the parable of the builders in Matthew 7:24-27.

Father, teach us to be wise builders.

Time Travel

Pull out old yearbooks, family photo albums, baby books, preschool drawings, and the like. Gather everyone on a cozy evening and take some time reminiscing about days gone by.

See if you can spot clothes you'd never wear again or remember the stories that accompany particular pictures. Sometime during the expedition, have everyone finish this sentence, "One thing I'll always remember about my past is . . . " Afterward, shuffle off to bed and "time travel" into tomorrow on the vehicle of sleep.

Thanks for the memories of you, Jesus.

164
Put Up Traffic Signs in Your Home

If your house is like ours, you probably need them anyway! How about a "Merging Traffic" sign in the hallway, "Stop" on the refrigerator, "Slow" at the dinner table, "No Outlet" on a bedroom, "Scenic Route" on a bathroom, "Loading Zone" at the garage entrance, and so on. If you really need it, let family members take turns being traffic cop and issuing "tickets" to people guilty of moving violations!

Lead us in the path of righteousness for your name's sake, Lord Jesus.

165
Smell

Take a walk around the block and list everything you smell. Is that bacon frying at the Findleys' house? Are the honeysuckles blooming on the corner? Does that car need a new emissions test? What kind of perfume was that girl who passed you wearing? See if each person can list at least 10 things. Then go home and takes showers—someone else who read this book may be smelling you!

Heavenly Father, may our family be like a sweet fragrance today.

166
Conduct a Soft-Drink Taste Test

Test your soft drink savvy with this creative spark. Pour several different soft drinks into opaque glasses, then cover and mix up the glasses so no one know which glass contains which drink. Next gather everyone and have them sip a taste out of each cup, writing down guesses of which soft drink brand they think each is. When everyone is ready, compare your guesses to see who got the most correct. Ask yourselves: Why do you suppose God gave us a sense of taste? How would life be different without it?

Today, Lord, help us to taste and see that you are good!

167

Draw on a Family Member's Belly

Use washable markers for this ticklish art project. See if you can complete a whole picture without making your "canvas" giggle! This spark is especially fun on hot summer days when your family's all going swimming anyway.

Give me a reason to smile today, Jesus.

168

Experiment with Food Coloring at Breakfast

Why simply read about green eggs and ham when you can eat them? Or even better, why not eat blue waffles in orange syrup? As long as you've got a few drops of food coloring, you can make any breakfast exciting—just like Dr. Seuss! One warning, though: Yellow pancakes are just *not* appetizing. Believe us. We know.

Father, start our day today with a glimpse of you.

169

Use Colored Light Bulbs for a Day

There's at least one really cool thing about living in America: tinted light bulbs. Find a local store that has light bulbs in all kinds of colors. See what life in your home might be like with different colors in charge. Try a green bulb in your bedroom, a red one in the kitchen, blue in the bathroom. Compare how "coloring" your house colors your view of life as a whole. Then, just as a reminder of your experience, put a different colored bulb in your porch light for the next few weeks.

God, please color our day with your creativity and grace.

170
Go Limerick-Wild

A limerick is a five-line poetic device in which lines one, two and five rhyme with each other, while lines three and four have their own separate rhyme. Use this silly device to wax poetic about each person in your family. Here's our humble attempt at limerick madness: "There once was a boy named Tony/Who rode on a horse that was bony/They rode down the street/Got pizza to eat/And now he has a fat pony!" OK, your turn!

Jesus, let us express our devotion to you in many different ways this week.

171
Leave an Etch-a-Sketch™ by the Phone

Pamper your creative flow by leaving a "doodling outlet" by the phone. With an Etch-a-Sketch™ you have the challenge of drawing in connected lines and the security of knowing you can quickly erase any unflattering examples of your skill. Let your phone conversation be your guide for what to draw. For example, if you're stuck in a discussion about the latest *TV Guide*, you could draw a big, yawning face. In an intimate examination of the strengths and weaknesses of your favorite football team, you could draw a helmet and logo. So go ahead and be a doodle bug, just remember someone could be looking over your shoulder!

God, etch your character into the heart of each person in our family.

172

Arrange Flowers

Launch into the wilderness (OK, go out back) and collect a sample or two of every flower you see. Bring all your samples inside, put a vase in the middle of the table, and let everyone make small and large contributions to a floral arrangement masterpiece. Set the centerpiece in the middle of the table at dinnertime so you can admire your work. (Hey, if it's really good, you could start a family florist shop and make millions!)

Thank you, Creator, for decorating our world with flowers.

173

Write a Love Song

Take the easy way out, though. Pick a tune you really know well (such as the *Brady Bunch* theme song or "I'm Just a Bill" from *Schoolhouse Rock*), and write new words to the old tune. Make your lyrics good and sappy, full of romantic language, and so sweet they make your loved one pucker up for a kiss!

Let me love my family more each day, dear Father.

174

Make New Words from Family Names

Another good one for travelers! Make a list of the names of everyone in your family, then see who can use letters from those names to create the most new words. Some of our attempts included wondrous words like . . . "Maim" "Note" and "Key." (OK, we never claimed to win any spelling bees.) Surely you can do better than we did, so go ahead and make those words!

Heavenly Father, let our lives be a good reflection of your name.

Mike and Amy Nappa

175
See the Music

All those people who select soundtracks to your favorite movies had to get their starts somewhere. We figure your living room is as good a place to start as any. Gather the family and listen to a movie soundtrack. As a song is playing, brainstorm the "scenes" that should go with the music if it were to be included in a movie. A rowdy, bouncy song might be the background for a merry-go-round. A sweet, gentle orchestra could be a solo dance in an empty hall. Use your imagination and "see" the music.

Lord, you are awesome. Let us sing your praise this week.

176
Assign Colors to Represent the Weather

Think of it—you can make your own family code to the weather forecast! Decide what colors go best with what weather conditions, like "charcoal" for cloudy, "white" for snow, or "blue" for rain showers. Then the next time one of you wants to know what the weather is like outside, you can say something like, "Partly charcoal with a possibility of white or scattered blue later today!"

Rain blessings into our home today, Lord Jesus.

177
Look Under a Rock

No need to explore outer space to find new worlds—there's usually a universe hidden under a nearby rock or brick. Tumble one over and see what's there. Chances are you'll find a worm or a beetle or at least some really cool fungus. If you take a stick and dig around, you might also find some other interesting creatures hidden just beneath the surface. (Warning: Check with Mom or Dad before you bring anything into the house!)

Let me discover something new about you today, God.

178
Wear One Glove All Day Long

Back in the 1980s, Michael Jackson started a fad of wearing one glittered glove during concerts. You don't need to do anything nearly as extravagant (or trendy). Slip on a glove in the morning and wear it all day. See how adding this little layer of fabric to your hand changes your day. Afterward, ask yourself: Why in the world did people think this was cool when Michael Jackson did it? What creative adjustments did you make to overcome your slight disability? (If you're feeling really gutsy, try wearing a mitten tomorrow!)

Lord, help me be sensitive to others today.

179
Bury Treasure

Put a handful of coins in a bag, wrap it up tightly in a larger bag, and then bury it somewhere on your property. Mark the spot with some slightly unique (but not too obvious) marker. Then make a "treasure map" with cryptic symbols and only marginally difficult clues telling how to find the treasure. If you want, make up some story (to accompany the map) about pirates who buried the treasure years ago. When it's all ready, crumple the map to make it look old, and you might even singe the edges with a match. Then leave the map and a few digging tools to be found by your family!

Remind me each day, God that my loved ones are the greatest treasure you've given me on this earth.

180
Create an Orchestra Out of Kitchen Utensils

It's time to raid the kitchen—but not for food. Have everyone look for anything they could use to make music. For example, you might commandeer a pot and a wooden spoon (for a drum), glasses filled with different levels of water (for chimes), a handful of flatware (for rubbing together as percussion), and so on. After you've each got an "instrument," hold a family jam session to see what kinds of beautiful music you can all make together!

Let us make a joyful noise to you, Lord!

181

Make a Thumbnail Sketch on a Styrofoam™ Cup

We've all done this at one time or another, used our fingernails to etch out a drawing on the side of a cup of coffee or punch. Just imagine what you can do if you put your mind to it! Give everyone a Styrofoam cup, a fingernail file (if needed), and five minutes to create the best fingernail art possible. After five minutes are up, compare your masterpieces and vote to see which is the family favorite. And since you've got the cups out, go ahead and enjoy a nice hot cup of cocoa as well.

Make each person in this family a masterpiece in your sight, dear Father.

182

Select Songs for the Soundtrack of Your Life

Imagine they were making a movie of your life, and gave you the responsibility to choose the background music. What would be on the car stereo as your parents rushed to the hospital when it was time for you to be born? What band would be playing as you made your way to your first day of school? Who serenades the moment of your first kiss? Pick all your favorites, and put them on a tape in case your life needs a little background music sometime in the future!

Jesus, fill my life with happy, heavenly music.

183
Spend a Day without Speaking

Can you do it? You might as well try! (Allow yourself one slip-up, just in case.) See if you can go from breakfast until dinner without saying a word. Communicate through body language, facial expressions, written notes, sign language, charades, whatever. See what kind of radical impact that has on your daily life. At dinner, have everyone complete this sentence: "One important thing I learned today is . . . "

Let us hear your still small voice in the silence of our day, Lord.

184
Sponsor a Men's Dessert Bake-off

Originally invented as a chance for Mike to show he could actually cook something, this has become an annual tradition at our house ever since. (Last year, Mike pulled off a cheesecake!) Invite a few families over for a cook-out, and require every adult male to bake a dessert as his family's admission to the feast. No female hands may touch the dessert or its ingredients until it's judging time! Allow everyone (kids included) to taste test each desert and vote on their two favorites. Tally the votes and give the top vote-getter the coveted, yet elusive, Plastic Spatula Award (a spatula with a ribbon on it).

God, help us appreciate the unique gifts you've given each of us.

185
Sculpt Ice

Buy a block (or several blocks) of ice from your local grocer. Bring the ice back home and put it in a cool, shady place that can get wet. Next, pass out screwdrivers and gloves to family members (have older people supervise younger ones) and begin chipping away to create an ice sculpture. See if you can carve simple, yet distinct figures such as a horse, a happy face, or a baseball bat. When you're all done, take a picture to remind you of your Michelangelo-like talents.

If you can't get ice blocks from your local grocer, try this: Fill an empty half-gallon milk carton with water and leave it overnight in your freezer. The next morning, peel away the carton to reveal your own, homemade ice block!

Father, chip away whatever is not right in my life.

186
Spend a Day on Crutches

Borrow or rent a pair of crutches, then go through your daily tasks pretending as if you have a broken leg (you can choose which leg). See if you can discover new ways to increase your personal "speed limit" while walking on the crutches. Time how long it takes before your armpits get sore. Keep track of how many things you accidentally knock over with your crutches. At the end of day, thank God for giving you the gift of mobility in life.

God, teach me to lean on you as I walk through this life.

187
Design a Device to Make Your Bed

There are a lot of great inventions in this world, but for some reason no one has yet invented a Bed-Maker. That means there's still time for you to amaze the world with your inventor skills and keep Mom from complaining about your messy covers at the same time. Use your imagination and "invent" a robot who sole purpose is to make a bed. What kind of attachments will it need? How many arms? What will it use for folding? for fluffing pillows? Draw a diagram of this dream machine and show it to your Mom. Maybe she'll be so excited about it that she'll forget to remind you to make your bed today.

Lord, let me see the endless possibilities you've created for my life.

188

Count Your Blessings

Figure out how many days have passed in this year so far, then as a family, brainstorm as many things for which you have to be thankful as there are days spent. For example, on April 11 you'll want to brainstorm 101 blessings in your family's life. (It's OK if you need more than one sitting for this creative spark idea.) Don't be overwhelmed by a seemingly large number—you'll be surprised at how active God really is in blessing your life!

Heavenly Father, open our eyes to see the many ways you bless us.

189

Create a Superhero

Wouldn't it be cool if you had the ability to stretch your neck like a giraffe, swim like a dolphin, leap like a frog, and race like a cheetah? You could be Animal Man (or Animal Woman)! OK, so you can't really do those things, but you can invent a superhero who would be able to. Think of any cool powers your hero could have, and use colored pencils to draw that hero in his or her full costume. You might even want to dress up as that hero for trick-or-treating this year!

Jesus, let me remember I don't have to be super to be like you.

190

Invite a Bible Character to Dinner

Take turns dressing up as your favorite Bible characters and role-playing as if that character has come over to join you for dinner. Prepare food your character would probably want, and be sure to read up on your chosen character before role-playing. Have a question-and-answer time when you tell other family members all about your character (yourself) and what you "remember" about your life as a Bible hero or heroine.

Dear Lord, give us a never-ending appetite for the discoveries to be found in the Bible.

191

Use Every Fifth Word

Take a magazine article and highlight every fifth word from the beginning to the end of it. Next, write the words you highlighted on a separate sheet of paper, and somehow write a story that uses every one of those words. You may work as a group, with every family member taking turns adding a new sentence, or as individuals, with every family member making his or her own story. When you're done, compare your stories to the original article to see how you've improved it!

Jesus, help us become a family that thinks beyond the ordinary.

192

Make a Crossword Puzzle

Those crossword puzzles in the paper are too hard (or too easy!) anyway. So cut out the puzzle part, but leave off the clues. Photocopy the blank puzzle, and then make your own words and clues for the spaces provided. Fill in one of your copies with the answers, and leave the other blank. Use clues specific to your family such as "A five-letter word for that place we vacationed at last year." When it's all ready, hand off the blank puzzle and its clues to the rest of the family and see if they can complete it correctly.

Unravel the mysteries of your love for me, Lord, and use me to help unravel them for others.

193

List Aromas You Associate with Holidays

They say that the sense of smell is the one that makes the strongest imprint on our memories, and we maintain that every holiday has its unique aroma. See if we're right by listing all the aromas your family associates with particular holidays. For example, Thanksgiving for us smells like turkey roasting in the oven and pumpkin pie cooling on the counter. What does Thanksgiving smell like at your house? or Christmas? or Independence Day? or your birthday? See if you can sniff out the answers!

God, thank you for giving us noses—and good-looking ones at that!

194
Place a Price Tag on Everything in Your Room

Think of it as estate planning! Set a value on everything in your room—bed, pictures, clothes hanging in the closet, socks under the bed, and more. Allow yourself only three "priceless" stickers, meaning only three items are so valuable no amount of money could buy them. When you're done, total up all the prices and then impress your family with your "net worth."

Thank you, Jesus, for considering me valuable.

195
Picnic in the Living Room

Picnics are great . . . except for the weather, and the ants, and the sand that always gets in your sandwiches. So why not picnic in the comfort of your home? Pack a huge basket filled with your favorite picnic items like egg salad sandwiches, chips, cookies, fruit, and chilled sodas. Then trek all the way to your living room, spread a blanket out on the floor, and have an outdoorsy feast indoors! (For extra fun, take along a Nerf™ flying disk and play catch in the house!)

Let us feast on the joy that comes from you today.

196
Create a Comic Strip

Look through the Sunday comics in your local newspaper to get some ideas, then draw your own four-panel comic strip (stick figures are OK). Think of a few fun characters (like a talking monkey or your big brother in long johns), add a silly situation (like a trip to the moon or a lumberjack contest), and giggle your way through the drawings and captions. If it's really funny (and your big brother doesn't beat you up), send it to your local paper and ask them to print it!

Thank you, God, for the gift of laughter.

197
Make a Maze in Your Living Room

Use masking tape to "draw" a maze of corridors all over the living room floor. Include a few dead ends, a few corridors that simply go around in circles, and one slightly disguised route that goes from one end of the living room to the other. Use mazes in activity books for examples of what you can do. When it's all done, offer your loved ones a hug each if they can get from start to finish within 10 seconds!

Father, please never let me lose sight of your will for my life.

198
Find the 10 Best Excuses for Being Late

You never know when you might need these, so they're good to keep on hand. Poll several of your friends and family members to discover the most outlandish, real-life excuses they used (or heard being used). For example, Amy's brother once told his Mom he was late getting home from a date because they were held hostage at the restaurant. Of course his mother didn't believe such a wild tale—until she saw the hostage crisis reported on the evening news! If you get 10 really exceptional excuses, send them off to David Letterman. Maybe he'll use your list on his show!

No matter what, dear God, please don't let excuses get in the way of my relationship with you.

199

Write a Love Note Using Magazine Words

Write a brief love note to your spouse, but instead of using your own handwriting, write them ransom-note style. (Tell your spouse it's because he or she has taken captive your heart!) Clip words out of magazines that say what you want to say and paste them in the correct order onto a sheet of stationary. Leave your love note on someone's pillow tonight before you go to bed.

Lord, give me just the right words to express my love.

200

Go by a Pseudonym for a Day

Hey, famous writers do it, and so do rock stars, movie actors, and others. So why not you? Pick a pseudonym or pen name you like and pretend for a day that that's your name. Write it on your homework, insist that everyone call you that name, order pizza under that name, and while you're at it, go ahead and write a bestseller under that name as well!

Father, thank you for knowing my name!

201

Reorganize Your Kitchen Cabinets

Wreak havoc on your kitchen routines! Take everything out of the cabinets, and then restock the cabinets according to this one rule: Nothing can return to its original position. Move the flatware to the junk drawer, put the plates the glasses cabinet, put the pots and pans in the pantry. Leave the new arrangement for at least a week—or until you finally stop surprising yourself by what you find behind a cabinet door.

Lord, reorganize our priorities until you are truly first in our lives.

202

Go Pocketless (or Purseless)

You'll be amazed at how much you've come to depend on those little hiding places sewn into your jeans. Don't believe us? Try doing without pockets for a day. Or, try going without your purse. Where will you keep your keys? Your money? Other miscellaneous items? Use your creative mind to figure that out today! Afterward, gather your family members to share your discoveries from the day.

Teach us to depend more on you each day, O Lord.

203

Give a Prize to the 10th Person You See Wearing Yellow

We've all heard of department stores giving out random prizes to the "millionth customer," so why not give out a random prize to someone you come in contact with today? Select a small prize (such as a candy bar or fast-food gift certificates), and have each family member carry an example of that prize through his or her day. Award your prizes to the 10th person you see wearing yellow, the 20th person who smiles at you, or some other random choice. Tell each other about your "award ceremonies" at the end of the day.

Jesus, let our prizes encourage the people who need a lift today.

204

Spend $10 Million

Aaah, to dream. That's one of life's great pleasures. Gather the family, pretend you've won the lottery, and dream about how you'd spend $10 million. Would you buy a mansion? Get his and hers Rolls Royces? Hire a maid and chauffeur? Buy the local video game store? Pay for all seniors at your local high school to go to college? Take your time and enjoy spending your millions. After all, this could be the only time when spending money is free!

Let us always spend our money—no matter how much we have—on things that you care about, God.

205
Spend $1.37 (No More, No Less)

Give each family member an envelope with $1.37 in it, then take the whole crew to a nearby grocery or discount store. Challenge everyone with the task of spending exactly that amount of money in their envelopes (no more, no less) on items in the store. Give family members only 13 minutes to make their purchases (have younger children accompany older family members during this excursion). Meet at the door afterward and compare cash receipts to see who got the closest to the goal (tax included!).

Father, help us manage our family budget wisely—and have fun at the same time.

206
Plan the Perfect Day

Gather the family on a Friday night and ask the question: If, as a family, tomorrow we could do anything at all within reason, what could we do that would make it a perfect day for everyone? Brainstorm ideas and plan a whole day from waking to bedtime. Then get up the next morning and do it! If it turns out to be not quite as perfect as you'd hoped, try brainstorming again next Friday night. Keep at it until you find "the perfect day."

Father, help us appreciate the time we spend together, even in less than perfect circumstances.

207
Make a Kite from Scratch

Go to a local store and examine the kites. Check out sizes, styles, and materials. Then go home and pull together an assortment of supplies that you estimate can be used to build a kite from scratch. Draw out your design for a kite on a sheet of paper and build the real thing! When it's ready, take it outside and see if it'll fly. (Be prepared to make last minute repairs or changes to you design!)

Jesus, let me soar with you today!

208
Find the Most Extraordinary Thing at a Park

Take a trip to a local park. In between flying on the swings and playing catch on the grass, stop to look for something extraordinary. Perhaps you'll find a robin's egg, or a silver dollar buried in the sand. Have each family member share at least one extraordinary thing with everyone else before you end your time at the park.

Thanks for making our family something extraordinary, God!

209
Make Jewelry out of Breakfast Cereal

Insist that parents buy the sugary sweet cereal for this idea (you know what to do if there's any left over, of course). See what creative kinds of jewelry you can make using sugary sweet cereal as the "jewels." Try stringing Froot Loops™ on yarn to make a bracelet, or gluing Cocoa Puffs™ on a stick-pin to make a broach for Mom. Let your creative energies run wild to see if you can make a ring, necklace, hair comb, and earrings as well. Give the best items to your parents as a gift.

Decorate my life with your love, dear God.

210

Wear the Jewelry Your Kids Make for You

Even if it's made out of breakfast cereal! (Who cares what they say about you at the office anyway?)

Heavenly Father, thank you for the gift of one another.

211

Color

This will be a return to childhood for some family members. Go to the store and have each family member choose a coloring book to be his or her very own. Then head home, spill out a box of crayons, and spend some time coloring pictures from your books. Do the best job possible, and be creative in your use of colors. When you're all done, tear out a colored page from each of your books and tape the pages to the refrigerator for display.

Let us be the ones, dear Lord, who get to color outside the lines of life!

212

Wear Earplugs for a Day

Trust us, you'll want to use the foam kind that airport workers wear (the rubber ones hurt after you wear them for any length of time). Put your earplugs in at breakfast, then go through the rest of your day as a hearing-impaired individual. See what kind of adjustments you must make to cope with normal daily activities. See how others who aren't hearing impaired treat you. At the end of the day, ask yourself: How will my experience today change my attitudes or actions in the future?

Holy Spirit, speak to my heart, not just my ears.

213
Go to a Movie Incognito

Celebrities have to do this all the time—put on a disguise to avoid being mobbed by their adoring fans. Imagine that yours is a well-known family who just wants to have a night out without being pestered for autographs. Select "disguises" for each family member (such hair up in a hat, dark sunglasses, trench coats, fake mustaches, and so on). When everyone is dressed up, go out for a movie, staying "incognito" for the whole evening. (If you see someone who recognizes you, go ahead and give them an autograph!)

It's no secret that we love you, Lord!

214
Shave in the Opposite Direction

Do you typically shave from up to down or down to up? Whichever it is, do the opposite today (allow yourself a few minutes extra in the bathroom this morning!). If you're really feeling gutsy, start on the opposite side of your face, or on the opposite leg (whichever is appropriate). Afterward, ask yourself: Why does making one minor change like this make an impact on my whole shaving experience?

(Note: Our facial-hair-empowered editor wants a substitute option for those of you who, like him, never pass a razor across your face or legs. So here it is: Try shaving a balloon instead! See which direction is least likely to pop the balloon—up, down, sideways, diagonal, or in circles. Afterward, ask yourself: Why does changing the shaving direction on a balloon impact whether or not it pops?)

Help me know, Father, how to walk in the same direction you're leading.

Sample Everything at the Grocery Store

Many discount grocery stores set up tables on weekends to encourage their customers to sample various sale items. This Saturday, take your family to one of these stores and sample everything, no matter how bizarre it may look or smell. You'll expand your tasting horizons by leaps and bounds! (After all, there's a reason they're giving this stuff away.) When you're done, vote on the best-tasting sample item, then go back and buy a package of it for "sampling" at home later.

God, help us find something new that we actually like today.

Sit in a Different Pew

Much as we hate to admit it, our church-going can turn into a rut. Next Sunday, break out of the rut by sitting in a different part of your church. Try the balcony, or the left side against the wall, or right down front, or way in the back—anywhere as long as it's not your usual seating area. During the service, ask yourself: How does this different perspective change my experience in this church service?

Thank you, Father, for being wherever we are.

Visit a Different Sunday School Class

If your church is like ours, your Sunday school classes are very much segregated by age: adults go to one class, teenagers to the youth group, children to kids' church, and so on. Mix things up a bit this week by visiting different Sunday school classes, just to observe. A teenager might visit the senior citizen's class, an adult could visit the third-graders, and an elementary child could visit the youth group. Gather everyone for lunch and a discussion on how all these classes are unique.

Change our outlook on life today, O Lord.

Mike and Amy Nappa

218
Read a Different Bible Translation

Admit it. Sometimes reading the Bible just gets boring. (It's OK, it happens to everyone.) If you find you're in an extended "dry" period where nothing in the Bible seems interesting, maybe it's time for a new perspective. Try reading the same passage in several different translations, or switch translations completely for a while. For example, if you normally read the King James Version (KJV), try reading the New Living Translation (NLT), or the New International Version (NIV). Jot down any new insights you gain from your reading and share them with a friend.

Father, thank you for writing a love letter to me.

219
Find Three Magazines You Never Knew Existed— and Read Them

Hit the library or local magazine stand. Search the shelves until you find three magazines you didn't know existed. Is there something called *Sheep Monthly*? or *Lego*™ *Lovers Magazine*? You'll never know until you look! Once you find three magazines you're unfamiliar with, take time to read them as thoroughly as possible. Look for at least one new bit of trivia from each magazine that you can share with the family today.

Today, let me discover something about you, Jesus, that I never knew before.

220
Rent the Video Recommended by the Clerk

At your local video rental store, ask the clerk to recommend the best family movie he or she has seen. Keep asking for recommendations until the clerk names one your family hasn't seen—then rent it! (You may have to ask more than one clerk for suggestions.) Promise the clerk a tip if the video turns out to be as good as he or she says it is. (If it is good, take back a coupon good for a free ice cream at a local ice cream parlor along with the video when you return it.)

Help us follow your recommendations for life that we find in the pages of the Bible, God.

221

Host a Tailgate Party—in Your Driveway

Want to enjoy the festivities of the big game, but don't have tickets? You can host a tailgate party in your driveway, and be done in time to watch the game on TV in the comfort of your home. Set up a grill, a few lawn chairs, some coolers filled with soft drinks, plenty of chips, and dessert behind the bumper of your car at home. Invite a few friends over, dress in team colors, and declare yourselves the Satellite Tailgate Party for the game.

Dear Father, please join us today as we party in the driveway!

222

Switch Toothpastes

OK, now we're meddling. But even though we realize how easily a family can get attached to a certain toothpaste, sometimes you gotta take a risk! Next time you're in the toothpaste aisle at the store, pick up a new brand or flavor to try. (We recommend the Colgate kids' flavor!) Try it for a week, just to see if you get used to it. Gauge whether or not you're brushing more, less, or about the same since the change. (And if it's really bad, you can "accidentally" lose the unfinished tube in the nearest trash can!)

Please bring freshness to our spirits this week, Jesus, and smiles to our faces.

223
Play "Connect the Stars"

On a clear night, go outside to gaze at the sky. Play "connect-the-stars" to create new constellations. See if you can draw imaginary lines between the stars to make the shape of your home, your cousin's left ear, a cocker spaniel, or anything else you think of.

God, how majestic you are!

224
Take an Art Class

Did you know that every color is numbered? One shade of green is called "Pantone 361." If you had taken an art class recently, you might have know that for yourself. Enroll in an art class at a local community college and see what else you can learn. (And if you get to be really good, tell our publisher you want to design our next book!)

Lord, never let me feel too old to learn something new.

225
Take a Craft Class

OK, so you don't feel really artsy, but you like making things with your hands. Then skip the art class and enroll in a craft class. The fun thing about these classes is you get to go shopping for craft supplies as part of your schoolwork. And, you can use your home-work for a present!

Lord Jesus, unleash the creative "craftiness" hiding inside me!

226
Take a Creative Writing Class

Of course, how could we be writers if we didn't include this idea in the book? We're not talking about taking one of those boring classes where you write research papers. We think you should take a class that makes you use your imagination in conjunction with your writing skills. One of those classes where your assignments are things like "write a story about a leprechaun" or "imagine you survived the sinking of the *Titanic* and write what happened." If one of your stories turns out particularly well, make copies and share it with friends and family.

Fill my mouth with words of praise for you, Creative God.

227
Take a Dance Class

One more, and then we'll stop badgering you to further your education. As long as you're exercising your mind in the previously mentioned classes, you might as well exercise your bodies as well. And besides, graduation from this class gives you an excuse to take a loved one on a date to show off what a great student you are!

Lord, make me a dancer as good as David was!

228
Eat Dinner at Five Different Restaurants—
All in One Night

Separate your meal into five courses (such as appetizer, soup and salad, main dish, side dishes, and dessert). Then select the best restaurant in town for each of these courses and hop in your car for dinner at all five places! Eat the appetizer at the first restaurant, soup or salad at the second, and so on. When you're finally stuffed and through dessert, waddle your way home and rate one restaurant as "The One We'd Most Like to Eat an Entire Meal At." Plan to go there in the near future.

Our generous Creator, we thank you for (among other things) the ability to taste and enjoy food!

229
Have a "Most Creative Dive" Contest

At your next swim party, put on a contest to see which family member can display the most creative dive off the board. Give each person three entries, and encourage them to go all out in their presentations. For example, contestants may want to do a "Standing O" dive (a jump with both arms forming a circle overhead), an "Elvis" dive (a dive with a hip wiggle), or something else entirely. Award points for both originality and execution. Don't do anything too dangerous!

Dear Lord—no belly busters please!

230
Make a Page for an "I Spy" Book

Walter Wick and Jean Marzollo have created a wonderful series of books called the "I Spy" series. In each book, Wick has assembled a menagerie of items crammed into a small space, and photographed it to make a page. The reader then must search to find certain items on that page for which Marzollo has given clues. So, first check out one of these books at the library or pick one up at a local bookstore to get a feel for what they do. Then, gather your own menagerie of objects, arrange them decoratively and take a photograph of them yourself. When the photo is ready, write up clues for your family members and see how long it takes them to discover the items you've spotlighted in your photo!

When I need you, Jesus, please find me.

Go Barefoot

Hey, it was good enough for Moses, so why not your family? See if you can spend a whole day without the luxury of shoes. (Saturdays in the spring are usually best for this.) Plan outings that don't require shoes, and be sure to watch for broken glass or stickers in the grass! Afterward, ask yourselves: What was great about going barefoot? What was not so great? How would I survive if our family couldn't buy shoes at all?

Thank you, Lord, for giving us the ability to feel grass between our toes!

232

Toss Water Balloons off the Roof

A few years ago, David Letterman caused quite stir by tossing odd things off the roof of his television studio. Now, we don't want you to start tossing watermelons and TV sets off your roof, but it is pretty interesting to toss water balloons from the rooftops. Get a ladder and climb up to a flat area on your roof, then toss water balloons onto the ground below. See if you can hit a target (such as a crack in the driveway or a tree in the yard). See if the water stains on the ground form any unique pictures in your minds. When you're done, climb down and have a good, old-fashioned water balloon fight to finish. (Warning: DO NOT do this idea if climbing on your roof could put you or another family member in danger. Also, while you're on the roof, DO NOT throw balloons at people or animals; the added gravitational force could cause injury.)

Sprinkle a little joy in the sunshine of our family activities today, Father.

233

Switch the Colors in a Paint-by-Numbers Set

Have your parents get you one of those painting sets or coloring books that indicate which colors go into which portions of the pictures. Then ignore the directions! Use any color but the ones indicated to finish each picture. Who care if you end up with a yellow sky or a red dog? Make your pictures as colorful as possible. Afterward, ask yourself: How would my world be different if everything switched colors?

Help me to see all of the possibilities you've put in my life, Lord Jesus.

234
Assemble a Model without Looking at the Directions

Test your mechanical skill as well as sparking your creativity with this idea. Purchase a model from the store—the simpler the better. Then bring it home, throw away the directions, and see if you can assemble it so that it looks just as good as the picture on the box. Try to figure out where every piece goes (but it's OK if you have a few pieces left over.). Afterward, if you have enough money, buy another of the same model and put this one together using the directions. See if it turns out differently from the first one!

Help me to follow your directions as I put together my life, O God.

235
Rate the New Toys for Christmas

Family Fun magazine does this every year, but why should you depend on their subjective testing? You'd better check out for yourself which are truly the best toys for Christmas. Talk a parent into accompanying you to your local toy store, take along a notepad and a pencil, and begin testing. Walk down the aisles, making a note of the names of any interesting toys, their costs, and rating them from 1 to 10 (with 1 being "worthless," and 10 being "definitely ought to be under the Christmas tree.") When you're done, pass your list on to a parent. Maybe he or she will make good use of it.

Thanks for making fun a part of life, Jesus!

236

Talk in Rhyme All the Time
(or at Least during Dinner)

Play Dr. Seuss and see how often you can make your words rhyme during dinner. (You may want to keep a rhyming dictionary nearby in case someone draws a blank.) Feel free to help each other out in completing your rhymes. One word of caution, though: There is no rhyme for the word "orange!"

Holy Spirit, put good words in our mouths today.

237

Perform a Random Act of Kindness (or Two)!

Brainstorm ways your family can covertly perform acts of kindness for strangers—then spend a day doing just that! For example, you might donate books to the library, wash car windshields in a parking lot, pick up trash, buy a fast-food lunch for the fifth person behind you in line, or whatever. When you're done, discuss this question: How would our community be different if everyone were concerned about doing random acts of kindness?

Lord, help us be kind to everyone we meet.

238

Turn off the TV

Try it for a week. You may discover there's such a thing as "meaningful conversation!" (Plus it might give you time to try some of the other creative ideas in this book!)

Help us, Jesus, to find better things to do with our time than waste too much of it in front of the TV set.

Mike and Amy Nappa

Create Captions to Accompany the Photos in Your Family Album

Pull out a recent photo album and brainstorm captions to go along with pictures there. (This works especially well with vacation photos.) For example, the photo of Dad doing his creative dive might have the caption, "This is gonna hurt!" Or the photo of the family climbing a tree could say, "Call the fire department—we're stuck!" If you like, jot down a few of your favorite captions and paste them in next to the pictures for posterity's sake.

Father, help us see the humor in all of life's circumstances.

Make Your Own Stationery

Who says you have to be a big shot in corporate America to have your own letterhead? Certainly not us! Play around with graphics and text on a computer to create your own personal stationery letterhead. Use a symbol that reflects your personality (such as flowers, an American flag, or a sailboat), and print it out on colored paper. Use it for all your correspondence, or on notes you leave your family! If it turns out really well, send us a fan letter on it—we love mail! (See activity #365 for our address.)

Make my life a love letter to you, Jesus.

Look for Undercover Angels

The Bible tells us in Hebrews 13:2 that "some people have entertained angels without knowing it." That means there could be angels all around you today! See if you can blow their cover, or at least spot an angel or two. As you go through the day, look for people who seem especially kind, or who might be sharing a message from God. Who knows, they could be angels God has planted nearby in your life. At the end of the day, share with your family who you suspect might be the angels you saw today.

Lord, let others mistake us for angels this week!

242

Recycle

Dig through the trash around your house and find 10 things that you can somehow "recycle," or use again for a new purpose. Perhaps you can transform a milk carton into a toy, use crumpled paper for kindling in the fireplace, or spread eggshells as compost in the garden. Use your imagination to discover how you can avoid having to toss out these 10 items. If you come up with several creative ideas, share them with your local newspaper in a letter to the editor. Maybe they'll print it so everyone can benefit from your ideas!

Show us how to do our part to care for your creation, Lord.

243

Try on the Outfit Most Unlike You at the Clothing Store

You've been dressing like this for years, and since we're your friends, we figured it was our responsibility to get you to at least *try* something new. Take another family member, go to the mall, visit that clothing store you normally pass by, find an outfit that's most definitely not you, and try it on. Remember, you both have to try something on, so no unkind comments! If it actually looks good on, go ahead and buy it. So what if your friends and coworkers will think you've gone crazy (just smile and tell them you have!).

Jesus, daily give me courage to risk my life for you.

244
Plan a Surprise Party

You don't really need a reason. Make it a "We Love Dad" party, or a "You're a Great Sister" party, or whatever. Then make all your covert plans to carry off the party without the guest of honor knowing about it. What creative system will you use to get the invitations out? What innovative hiding place will you use to store the supplies? What ingenious technique will you use to get the guest of honor out of the house while you decorate? If you pull it all off, give yourself a pat on the back by throwing yourself a party next week!

It's no surprise, Jesus, we think you're wonderful!

245
Carry a Yo-Yo for a Day

Get a small, comfortable yo-yo and hang onto it for an entire day. Take it everywhere you go, but be careful not to break anything with it. See if you can learn three new tricks on it during the course of the day. Watch to find out when you're tempted to forget it. See how other people react to your having it. At the end of the day, ask yourself: What might it be like if everyone had a yo-yo attached to his or her hand for life?

Help me remember, Lord, that you're with me wherever I go.

246
Find out Why Five People Are Laughing

Your mission, should you decide to accept it, is to spot laughing people during your day and find out why they're laughing. Did someone tell a joke? Make a wisecrack? Slip on a banana peel? Watch a funny movie? Keep a record of your findings and share them with your family at dinner tonight.

God, reveal to us what makes you laugh.

Do the Same Homework Assignment as Your Oldest Child

Parents, don't let a child get away with saying, "You don't know what it's like for me!" Find out (in one way, at least) by tackling the same homework assignment he or she has. Is she writing a term paper on the causes of World War II? Then you write one, too. Is he bogged down in pages of algebra? You dive into the math book, too. Work together if you like, but no cheating! Afterward, try to talk your child into taking on one of your assignments at work.

Lord, give me a better understanding for the pressures children face and the ability to help them overcome.

248

Make a Sock Puppet that Looks Like You

Grab an old pair of socks, a marker or two, a mirror, and any buttons and thread you like for this idea. Study your face in the mirror for a while, then use your supplies to create a similar face on the toe of a sock. Use it later to put on a puppet show for your family. (If you're really good at this, make puppets that resemble other members of your family as well.)

God, thank you for making me, me!

249

Juggle

It's harder than it looks, but it's still possible. And if you get real good at it, you could become a clown and join the circus when you're older. Start by trying to juggle two balled-up socks with one hand. Once you've got that down, add a third sock and your other hand. After you've got all three socks going well, try substituting oranges or tennis balls. When you're 90 or so and can juggle all of these things, it'll be time to try out for the circus.

Jesus, I'm glad to know that nothing is too hard for you!

Order a Whopper™ with No Bun

Burger King prides itself on being able to fill orders to your preference, so put them to the test by asking for a Whopper with no bun. Mike tried this out for you, and yes they will serve them this way. His comments afterward were, "It's a little messy, but still tastes good nonetheless."

This week, Lord, help me find new ways to enjoy the simple things of life.

Coin a New Word that Means "To Eat Peanut Butter with Peas"

Hmmm, not as easy as it seems at first, huh? Well, don't worry, we know you can come up with just the right word. But you can't use "Epobee," 'cause we already coined that one. You can't use "Nutterotopy" either. (Same reason.) So what are you waiting for? Quit trying to copy our words and get busy making your own!

Jesus, you are too amazing for words, and I love you more than words can say.

Fill a Scrapbook with Your Favorite Cartoons

Every time anyone in your family spots a newspaper cartoon he or she finds particularly funny, clip it out and put it in a scrapbook. See how long it takes your family to fill up the book. Take some time to reread the clippings that have tickled your family's collective funny bone.

Lord, thanks for all the people who make us smile and laugh.

253
Choose a Family Mascot

How about an emu? Or Mickey Mouse? Or your family dog? Whatever it is, use it as a symbol and rallying point for your family. Challenge other families to fun competitions (like pie eating or bowling) and display your mascot in a prominent place during the competition. Once a year, have your very own "Family Colors Day" when everyone wears the colors of the mascot, and then attends a "Family Pep Rally" where you all cheer for each other by telling what you like about each family member.

Jesus, never let us forget your symbol of love and sacrifice— the cross.

254
Start a Book Club

Oprah Winfrey's got nothing on you! Corral a few of your friends who like to read and arrange to meet once a month to discuss a book. Take turns meeting at different people's houses, and let the host choose the book you'll all read. Be forewarned, however, people have largely different tastes in literature, so you'll probably end up reading a few good books and a few not-so-good ones! If you find one book that everyone absolutely loves, go ahead and send it to Oprah and ask her to use it for her show.

Thank you, Father, for the freedom to read many kinds of writings.

255
Create an Entry for *America's Funniest Home Videos*

What's something funny that your family does? Capture it on video and send it off to the show *America's Funniest Home Videos*! Make it something that everyone in the family has a part in (and you should probably include at least one big fall, too). Since you'll need to research the competition, gather the family to watch a few shows beforehand. Then, get those cameras safely rolling! (Don't forget to mention us if you make it onto the show!)

Thank you, God, for giving us the ability to laugh at ourselves.

256
Play "Never-Ending Story . . . "

"Once there was a family, and they tried a creative idea. Little did they know that . . . " Interested yet? Good! You finish the story— or another one of your choice! Gather the family, start a story by saying, "Once upon a time . . . " Then point to a family member to supply the next part. Have different family members supply new portions of the story until you've all had enough of the wacky adventures your creative minds dream up. (This is especially fun on long road trips!)

Lord Jesus, we know your love never ends, and for that we give you praise!

257
Make New Punch Lines for Old Jokes

Everyone's heard the opener, "Why did the chicken cross the road?" But not everyone knows the real answer: "To get away from old jokes!" (You may chuckle now.) Try out your comedic talents by creating new endings to old jokes. Test your creations on your family members (and remember, a groan is just as good as a laugh!). If you get some good ones, call Rosie O'Donnell and see if she'll read them on her show.

Lord, help me always remember that you are the one who completes my life.

Put on a Puppet Show with Plush Animals

Make special invitations for each person in your family, then at the appropriate time bring out your stuffed animal collection to put on a show. Invent a wild adventure for your animals (how about a treasure hunt across the seven seas?), then act out the voices for each one as it plays its part in the show. (If you have a lot of plush animals, get a brother or sister to lend you an extra pair of hands and a few extra voices to make the show a success.)

Jesus, following you is the greatest adventure of all!

259

Choose Your Outfit in the Dark

OK, first make sure it's a Saturday and that you're not leaving the house that day . . . then close your eyes and choose everything you'll wear for a whole day—without looking first to see what it is or even if it matches! Wear whatever you choose all day. Who knows, you might be the one to make dress shoes and golf shorts a really cool fashion fad.

Father, remind me that you care most about the appearance of my heart.

260

Brainstorm 10 Things to Do
While Waiting for a Movie to Start

We love movies—and hate waiting for them to start. If you're like us, then having a list of things to do can help banish those interminable moments of boredom while you wait for the lights to dim. Our list includes a quick game of "Never-Ending Story . . . " (see creative spark #256), tallying the total number of popcorn boxes in the theater, and trying to identify exactly what has spilled under the seat. Next time you're at the movies, start brainstorming your own list to see what 10 creative things you can . . . Oh, excuse us, please. The opening credits are starting to roll . .

We anxiously look forward to your return, and we pray that you would come quickly, Lord Jesus!

261

Add "House Rules" to a Game

Nobody ever said the only rules you have to play by are the ones in the box. Add your own "house rules" to any game, and up the "fun quotient" in the process. How about a standing ovation for anyone who rolls a seven? The person in the lead skips a turn every 15 minutes? Anytime a new player takes the lead, everyone sings, "She'll be comin' 'round the mountain when she comes"? Think of your best house rules. Then let the games begin!

Father, thank you for making us uniquely us.

262

Hide a Love Note for Another Family Member

Pour your heart out in a note to a family member. Then hide the note away someplace he or she will find it. You might leave the note in a purse, a sock drawer, a Bible, the medicine cabinet, a pants pocket, and so on. See how long it takes for your loved one to discover your note. (Warning: Sometimes notes are found by those they're not intended for—so don't write anything that could be used against you by crafty children!)

Grant me the ability, Lord, to love my family the way you love me.

263

Pray in Various Positions

Liven up your prayer life by experimenting with the way you pray. Try praying one night by kneeling by your bed. Another night, try laying face-down on the floor. Next try standing for the entire prayer time. Curl up in a ball another time. Check a concordance to see if you can find different postures of prayer used by people in the Bible as well. After your experiments, ask yourself: How did my posture affect my prayers? What can I learn from that?

I desire your presence, Lord. Meet me in my prayers.

264

Find the Ideal Place for a Secret Passageway in Your Home

There's always a secret passageway in mystery books, and never one in real life. We think it's time someone did something about that. Scope out your home to find the ideal place for installing a secret passageway. (We vote for one that goes from your room to the kitchen!) Check out every nook and cranny to make sure you've got the absolute best spot, then drop hints about how great a secret passageway would be for Christmas this year. (Maybe this'll be the year Mom and Dad finally give in!)

Jesus, you are the way to heaven, and I trust you to prepare a place for me there.

265

Dig for Definitions

Choose a word at random from the dictionary, then survey 10 of your friends to ask how they'd define that word. Write down all definitions. At the end of the day compare your friends' definitions with the actual one from the dictionary. See who was closest to the correct meaning, and also who was most creative in defining the word. Award them both a snack-size box of Alpha-Bits™ cereal!

God, you give meaning to our lives.

266
Give Your Loved One an Ink "Tattoo"

This was really cool in junior high, so it should be even more cool now, right? Take an pen and ink your name inside a heart shape somewhere on your loved one's body—you pick where! Wear your ink tattoo as a badge of love and pride (but you don't have to let anybody else see it if you don't want to.).

Lord, me plus you equals eternal love!

267
Collect a Dozen Clean Jokes

Some people collect baseball cards, others collect comic books. Why don't you start a clean jokes collection? Grab a sheet of paper and carry it with you everywhere you go today. Ask friends, family members, teachers, and others to share with you their favorite clean jokes. Write down any good ones to add to your collection. See if you can collect at least 12 good, clean jokes before the day's end. Here's our contribution: "Why did the boy throw his book in the ocean? He wanted some deep reading!" (Why aren't you laughing?)

Use me to make someone happier today, Jesus.

268
Host a Series of Bad Movie Nights

No, we're not talking about a night of X-rated movies (shame on you for thinking that!). We're talking about all those "B" movies that'd make filmmaker Ed Wood proud. Let each family member take turns picking out one video that you all know is going to be, well . . . stupid, but that somebody in the family wants to see anyway. Make it a rule that everyone has to watch at least 30 minutes of the chosen movie without complaining. (Our worst "Bad Movie?" Hands down it was Amy's choice: *The Pickle!*)

Heavenly Father, show us how to find good things in the midst of the bad.

Parents, Reenact Your Wedding for Your Children

Sure, they've seen the pictures and maybe even watched the video, but now you have a chance to let your children experience your wedding! Round up as many people as possible who were in your wedding, and let your children stand-in for people who aren't available. Then reenact your wedding ceremony for your kids. You can use your home or your church for the re-enactment. Order a wedding cake and have a full reception afterward. (Oh, and tell your kids they have to bring wedding gifts this time!)

Lord, we thank you for making us a family.

Write New, Personalized Wedding Vows

Now that you've reenacted your wedding (or if reenacting your wedding just isn't practical), take a few moments to write new, personalized wedding vows for your spouse. Reflect on your past years together and on what you hope to bring to your marriage in the years to come. Then share your new vows in a private ceremony on your next anniversary.

Father, grant our marriage love to last a lifetime and joy to last beyond the limits of time.

Quote Kipling

Just for fun, pick one random phrase from humorist and storyteller Rudyard Kipling, or another favorite writer, and quote it at odd moments during the day. Watch to see how people respond—and to see if anyone recognizes where the quote originated. Here are a few of our favorite Kipling quips: 1) "'Humph!' said the Camel; and the Dog went away and told the Man." 2) "And—which is more—you'll be a Man, my son!"

Lord, give me wisdom to know what's worth remembering—and what's not!

Mike and Amy Nappa

272

Decide Who Are the 10 Funniest People on Earth

Let everyone in the family vote for up to five different people. Choose only those candidates who truly make you chuckle and smile—and be sure you can prove it. For example, Robin Williams proves his "funny-ness" as the crack-up Genie in Disney's *Aladdin*. Tally up all your votes and publish your "10 Funniest People on Earth" choices in this year's Christmas letter to friends.

Thank you, God, for all the people who bring joy into our lives.

273

Make it BIG

Think of something your family really enjoys, then try to make the biggest representation of that thing as possible. For example, if your family is made up of ice-cream-aholics, make a giant, table-sized hot fudge sundae. Enjoy football? Host the world's largest Monday Night Football party. Can't get enough of flowers? Gather enough to make a door-sized bouquet for your house. After all, too much of a good thing is just about right!

Jesus, make us really BIG fans of you!

274

Doodle

Have each family member carry a doodle notebook every day for a week. Whenever you find yourself bored, distracted, or starting to yawn off, pull out the doodle notebook and pencil in a quick, meaningless sketch. At the end of the week, share your doodles with the family. Award the family member with the most sketches the not-so-coveted Doodle Bug Award (a plastic spider).

Use our doodling, Lord, to teach us something about ourselves.

275

Cast Your Family in a Fairy Tale

Imagine your acting talents have so wowed studio producers that they want your entire family to perform the leading roles in their next Fairy Tale Extravaganza movie. Which fairy tale will you choose? And who plays who if your family is cast in *Hansel and Gretel*? Or in *The Little Mermaid*? Or in *The Fisherman's Wife*? Feel free to read a few fairy tales to "bone up" on your roles.

Thank you, Father, that a happy family doesn't have to be a fantasy.

276

Recreate a Silent Movie

During the days of silent movies, a pianist played along while the movie ran, making appropriate background music to match the action. Recreate a silent movie in your own home with this creative idea. Turn on the TV set, but turn the volume all the way down. Then turn on the stereo and start scanning the stations until you find the perfect radio background to match the silent screen you're watching. Make silent movies out of as many TV shows as you like.

God, having you in my life is the best form of entertainment around!

277

Shoot a Roll of Film

Take a full roll of film and snap pictures of anything and everything that catches your eye today. Laundry swinging on the line look kind of neat? Snap a picture. See yourself in a mirror? Take another picture. Catch your Dad snoozing on the couch? Go ahead and capture that on film, too—but don't tell him we said to do it! After all your photos are developed, lay them out on the floor and make up a story that goes along with the finished pictures.

Lord, thanks for the memories!

278

Go on a Photo Scavenger Hunt

Have your family work together make a list of 10 to 20 creative scavenger hunt items, such as "a librarian," "something from Wal-Mart," "love" "the biggest star" and so on. Then grab a camera and start scavenging! (If possible, see if you can borrow an instant-print camera from a friend. If that's not possible, plan on taking your film to a one-hour photo shop for development.) Take pictures of as many items on your list as possible. Feel free to experiment with camera angles and picture poses. When you're done (and your film is developed) bring your pictures back to the house to look over. Then add a final item to your list: a shot of your family in front of your favorite ice cream parlor (Oh, go ahead and get a cone while you're there too!)

God, grant us the perceptiveness to recognize those "Kodak moments"—and a loaded camera nearby at just the right time.

279

Play with Your Food

You can make a wonderful face using rice, peas, and green beans, but unless you take a moment to play with your food, you'll never get to see it. Just once, for dinner, encourage everyone to mush their food around their plates to create unique and playful designs. Show off your artwork.

Thank you, great Father, for providing all our needs. Help us remember the needs of others.

280

Make Three Wishes

If a genie appeared and offered three wishes, would you be ready? (OK, so it's not going to happen, but it wouldn't hurt you to be ready, would it?) Imagine what you'd ask for to fulfill those three wishes. Assume you can't wish for more wishes, and you can't wish for something that would intentionally harm another person. So what would you wish for? Once you've decided, write a story titled, "The Three Wishes" about what might happen if your wishes actually came true.

In the end, Lord, my greatest wish is simply to know you better each day.

281
Grant a Wish

Make a coupon for each of your family members that reads, "Good for the granting of one wish that's within my ability to grant." Present each person with one of these coupons on a Friday morning and tell them they have 24 hours to make their wishes. Then spend all day Saturday granting their wishes.

Thank you, Jesus, for allowing me to grant another's wish.

282
Get in a Zone

For one day, designate the area around you as a "zone" of your own choosing. For example, you could be a hug zone, a no-complaints zone, a smile zone, a joke zone, a Disney zone and so on. Require that anyone entering your one must act out whatever you zone's theme is. At the end of the day, gather family members to compare stories about how people reacted to your zones.

Make our home a "Jesus zone" each day of our lives, O Lord.

283
Visit a Prison

Want to get a perspective change in a hurry? Call your local Prison Fellowship office and make arrangements to accompany their volunteers on a visit to a nearby prison. Make a mental list of all the things you take for granted that are "luxuries" for a prisoner. Inventory your feelings as you walk through the corridors of the prison and as you meet the inmates. Afterward, discuss your experience with the rest of your family.

Father, make your presence known inside the walls of America's prisons.

284

Create Your Family's Own *Little Instruction Book*

H. Jackson Brown Jr. has made millions selling his time-worn advice in the *Life's Little Instruction Book* series. But H. Jackson Brown Jr. has never met your family! Imagine that someone were going to join your family for a year, what would he or she need to know to make sure he fits into the way your family operates. Take an evening and brainstorm your advice for Jackson. Number each tidbit and put them all in a notebook titled, *Our Family's Little Instruction Book.* Make a copy for each family member to keep.

Lord, let our first instruction for life be to love you and to love each other.

285

Make Personalized Business Cards for Your Kids

Parents, affirm your kids just for who they are by having personalized business cards made for each of them. For example, if your son has a great sense of humor, is prone to get scrapes and bruises from playing outside, and loves fast food, his card could read as follows: "John Doe Jr. Professional laugher, bandage tester, and all-around great person. Accepts payment in cash or McDonald's coupons." Since turnabout is fair play, let your kids design new cards for you too!

Lord, use me to build my children's confidence in you.

Jump on the Bed

Contrary to popular opinion, beds were not made primarily for sleeping on. Rather, they were made first for jumping on, and then some bright soul figured out they could also be used for sleeping. (At least that's the way we heard it!) So, go ahead and use your parent's bed for its original purpose. (Get permission first.) See if you can jump high enough to touch the ceiling (but not bonk your head). Practice your trampoline jumps. If there's enough room, invite Mom and Dad to join in the fun!

Note: Our safety-conscious editor has informed us his mother would not approve of this idea, fearing someone might get hurt. If your parents, too, would be concerned for your safety while bed-jumping, please recruit them or other family members you trust to act as "spotters" who stand near the edges of the bed to make sure you don't fall off!

Father, please don't let the bed break!

Search for "Engaging Stories"

Every married person you know has an interesting story to tell about how he or she got engaged. Ask your parents for their story first, then ask teachers, family friends, older couples in your church, and anyone else you know who is married. Collect elements of the best ideas and use them as sparks to plan for your own creative engagement story.

When my time comes, Lord, give me an engagement story I can cherish forever!

Invent a Singing Telegram

You can actually make a living dressing up in goofy costumes and delivering silly messages in song to strangers. So, just in case your family needs a few bucks sometime, invent a singing telegram or two you all can deliver. Create your own unique costumes (clowns will work fine), and write up fun, lovebird lyrics to go along with a common tune. Feel free to add choreography and slapstick to the routine. When you're ready, take the show on the road and share it with friends or relatives.

Help us get in the habit of singing love songs to you, Jesus.

289

Create a Family Cookbook

You've all got your favorite foods, so compile them into the no-miss family cookbook. Let each family member contribute five recipes into each section—appetizers, snacks, main dishes, and desserts. Work together to write up the recipes, making sure to add any variations that make them just right for your family. Put all recipes in a notebook titled, *Our Family Cookbook*. Whenever someone in your family gets married, make sure his or her spouse gets a copy of this cookbook as well!

Heavenly Father, please include liberal amounts of love and respect in your recipe for our family.

290

Change the Message on Your Answering Machine

"You've reached 555-4444. We're not here right now, so leave a message after the beep." If this sounds even remotely like your current answering machine message, it's time for a change! Involve the whole family in a creative drama recorded for all who call while you're not home. Perhaps you've gone to meet the President, or maybe you're all busy with your Elvis impersonations (see #57). Remember, a good answering-machine message can entertain both you and your callers at the same time.

God, this is our message to you: We love you!

291

Perfect Your Imitations of Loony Tunes™ Voices

When Mel Blanc passed away several years ago, that left a huge void in the world of Loony Tunes™ voices. Oh sure, there have been pretenders who've tried to cover for the absence of Blanc's incredible skills, but none have been able to adequately fill the void. None, that is, until now. Yes, you and your family alone have the raw talent to aspire to Blanc's heights, so get busy practicing! Is there an Elmer Fudd among you? A Speedy Gonzalez lurking in your midst? You'll never know until you try. You may never make the Loony Tunes™ roster, but with a little practice, you can at least make really fun answering machine messages!

Give us opportunity today to imitate you in the lives of someone we meet.

292

Invent New Ice Cube Flavors

Nowhere is it written that all ice cubes must be water-flavored. Make a break from the norm by creating all-new flavors of ice cubes for your family. You might try standard Kool-Aid™ or juice cubes, or go all out and experiment with cola or chocolate soda ice cubes. Serve your frozen treat in the drinks for tonight's dinner!

Thank you, God, for always leaving room for something new in your world.

293

Have Church at Home

Just this once, we give you permission to skip church for a Sunday. Gather your family at home and hold a church service there instead. Choose family members to handle the different responsibilities of the service: someone to read scripture, lead in prayer, lead in singing, take the offering (which you can deliver to your church the next week), and someone to lead the family in a sermon and/or devotion. (Check out our book *52 Fun Family Devotions* if you're stuck for creative sermon ideas!) Afterward, discuss how your homespun church service compared to your regular service—then go out for lunch.

Lord, allow us to "have church" each day of the week and not just on Sundays.

294

Rap the Lyrics to a Country-and-Western Song

All right, it's true. Rap music and country-and-western music have absolutely nothing in common. That's what makes this such a great activity! Take the lyrics to a familiar country-and-western song, start a friend going on his or her best hip-hop beat, and then do your best rapper imitation as you work your way through the lyrics. (Be prepared to stop for uncontrollable laughter.) If you get a kick out of this, try singing lyrics to a modern rock song in your best opera voice!

God, thank you for inspiring such a wide variety of ways to praise you in song.

295

Eat Dinner Backwards

It won't kill you to eat dessert first for once, so go ahead and do it tonight. Eat the main dish next, and your salad or appetizer last. Afterward, ask: Why do you think we do things the same way over and over each day? What's something else we could do backwards tomorrow to give us a break in our normal routine?

Lord, dessert first is a blessing from you! Thank you!

296
Alphabetize Your Closet—
Just to See What it Looks Like

Empty all the clothes out of your closet, then rehang everything alphabetically by manufacturer. When you're finished, survey your work to see how it all turned out. Do you have T-shirts mixed in with dresses? Jeans next to suits? Or is it all about the same anyway? Keep your closet alphabetized for a week just to see if you get used to having it that way.

Lord, grant me new appreciation for the way you've provided for my needs.

297
Get Dressed in Alphabetical Order

Well, now that you've got your closet in alphabetical order, you might as well get dressed the same way. This could be tricky since "underwear" starts with a letter near the end of the alphabet (U), and "jeans" begins with a letter near the front (J)! That's where your creativity comes in . . . but you'll probably want to get up a little earlier just in case you need a few extra minutes to get fully dressed before you leave the house.

Father, help me to clothe my life with the character and personality of Jesus.

298
Take a U-Haul to the Movies

OK, they'll make you park on the back row, but you can still have a lot of fun nonetheless. Rent a moving truck on your way to the drive-in, pile a bunch of comfy pillows and a few sleeping bags in back, throw in some Chinese take-out and you've got the makings of the finest comfort this side of a limousine. Back the truck into place, open the cargo hold, get comfy in the back, and enjoy the movie. (If you're feeling Romanesque, move a couch and dinner table into the truck, and eat dinner while reclining and watching the movie!)

Mike and Amy Nappa

God, please don't let anyone in a big truck block our view of the movie screen tonight.

299
Start a Collection of Kids' Meal Toys

Why should your kids be the only ones who get entertainment along with their fast-food meals? Next time you buy your lunch, add on the kids' meal toy to your meal as well. Keep it up until you've got a collection of those little cars, movie characters, dolls, inflatable birds, and such to make any five-year-old jealous. Then surprise a five-year-old by giving him or her your entire collection so you can have an excuse to start all over again!

Father, let me keep the heart of a child always.

300
Have a "Family Members Only" White Elephant Exchange

Everybody loves white elephant exchanges at Christmas—that is, an exchange of gag gifts among friends. Where else can you wrap up some off-the-wall gift and actually have someone willing to receive it? Bring the fun home this year by having a "Family Only" white elephant exchange. Have each family member wrap up one unusual item from his or her room and bring to give. Number all presents from "1" to the total number of gifts, and have family members number off as well. Have person number 1 open the first gift, person number two open the second, and so on. Open the presents one at a time, and make it legal to trade gifts. Afterward, give yourselves one last gift and bake some fresh cookies to eat!

Lord, thank you for all the wondrous gifts you give to us, your family.

Audition for Community Theater

The point here is not necessarily to make the cast but to risk having others see your acting skills in action. So brush off those dramatic talents, contact your local theater for audition times, and move to center stage! Ask to read for any part that interests you. While you're there, pretend you're the director and rate all the competition yourself. Make your own cast list, then later see how it compares to the real director's choices. If you make the play, tell your family to ask for your autograph!

Lord, let me be concerned to impress you more than anyone else today.

302

Transform Your Lawn into a Sports Stadium

Use a bag of flour or powdered chalk to create mini-hash marks on the grass, set a row of lawn chairs off to the side, you've got a football stadium! Add a table with brownies and soft drinks, and your concession stand is in working order too. You're ready to challenge another family to meet you at the 50-yard line at high noon this Saturday, and to play a low-key game of touch football (using a Nerf™, of course). Add any handicapping rules as needed (for example, parents must hop on one leg, everyone older must freeze when a player under five carries the ball, and so on). Award the winning head of household a Gatorade™ shower!

Keep us all from injury, God, and may the best team win!

303

Make Your Own Fortune Cookies

Check out an Oriental cookbook from the library and find the recipe for making fortune cookies. Before you start baking, however, gather everyone at the kitchen table and write your best "fortunes" on little slips of paper. How about "Dad will soon give you $10" or "You are about to experience a family hug"? Use your homemade fortunes as the messages for your own brand of fortune cookies.

Jesus, because we can't know what the future holds, remind us to trust in you, the one who holds the future.

304
Rename the Colors in a Crayon Box

Whoever names crayons in real life certainly has an imagination. How else can you explain colors like "thistle," "bittersweet," and "melon"? What they don't know is that you have got more imagination than all crayon-namers put together! Just to prove it, take out a crayon box and think of all new names for every color represented. (If we're especially nice, will you name at least one crayon after us? Thanks!)

God, thank you for giving color to my world.

305
Make a Commercial for Mom's Cooking

Nobody cooks like Mom. Even macaroni and cheese tastes better when she makes it. That means you've got a hot commodity—Mom's cooking! Take a video camera, get together with all your brothers and sisters, and create a TV commercial advertising Mom or Dad's cooking. Add fun music, lots of testimonials, and scenes of happy people eating something from your parent's kitchen. Show the finished product to the family.

Help me today, dear Lord, to make my parents feel special.

306
Respell Your Name

This is the age of creative spellings anyway, so experiment to find a new way of spelling your name without changing the pronunciation. For example, instead of Amy, you might spell your name

Aimee, or Aymie, or even Aimi. For Mike you might spell your name . . . um . . . Mxyzptlk? (OK, so that one's a stretch, but you get the idea.) If you find a spelling you particularly like, use it for a while—we'll still know it's you.

Thanks, Jesus, for always knowing my name.

307
Give Your Pet a Makeover

Don't do anything that would harm your pet, but as long as it's safe, why not give your dog a new 'do, or your cat a new coiffure? Try curling an Afghan's fur, or food-color dying your kitty blue. Think about shaving the Jacksonville Jaguars emblem in your Doberman's fur, or painting your family initials on your pet turtle. If something turns out especially well, consider trying the same thing for activity #99!

God, bless all creatures here below.

308
Hold a Family Magic Show

Have everyone learn one or two different magic tricks for this one. You might check out a magic book from the library or pick up a magician's kit from a toy store. When you've each got your trick down to perfection, hold a family magic show. Take turns performing with great flourish each of your tricks. (Be sure to give each other properly grand introductions!) If you like, videotape the show and view it later to see if you can figure out how each trick was done.

Lord, let us never be fooled into believing you've stopped loving us.

Seatbelt a Stuffed Animal Next to You

Next time you have to go on a few errands, take along a friend—
your favorite (and preferably biggest) plush animal pal! Seatbelt
the stuffed buddy right in the seat next to you and let it go along
for the ride. See if anybody mistakes it for a real person, or if you
get any strange looks from other drivers thinking, "Why in the
world is there a plush animal seatbelted in that car?" If anybody
asks that question out loud of you, just tell them it's a top-secret
government experiment and drive merrily away!

Thank you, Jesus, for friends of all shapes and sizes!

310

Personalize Your Phone Number

How come only businesses get to have cool phone numbers like
"1–800–CALL–NOW" or "555–FUNN!"? We think it's time this
wrong has been righted, and you're just the person to do it. Look
at your home number on your phone receiver and make up a
memorable word using the letters that correspond with each number. (We have a friend who did this and came up with
"59–FROG–O." Surely you can do better.)

*Father, I'm glad you always hear me, no matter when I call you
in prayer.*

311

Go Head over Heels Tonight

Don't let yourself get into a sleeping rut. Try sleeping with your
head at the foot of the bed, just for one night. See if it makes a
difference, or if you have to make any other adjustments to com-
pensate (such as moving to the other side of the bed). Compare
stories with the rest of the family the next morning. Then have a
family bed-making party where you all pitch in to restore each
other's covers to normal!

Grant us all sweet dreams tonight, dear Lord.

Host an Academy Awards Party

When it's Academy Awards time, host your own private gala party event. Invite movie-loving friends to join you for an evening of watching the ceremonies. Have guests dress as their memorable movie characters (such as Scarlet O'Hara or Forrest Gump), and instruct each person to bring along a 30-second, academy style "acceptance speech." During commercial breaks, award your own Oscar parody awards to guests (such as Best Supporting Parent in a Family Series Who Regularly Lets Our Kids Hang Out at Their House). Cut off any guest whose acceptance speech goes too long by turning up the volume on the TV set!

Awesome God, no matter what the category, you are still—and always will be—the best of all!

Make a Puzzle out of Cookie Dough

Get a parent to help you with this, if you're not sure how to make cookie dough. Sugar cookies work best for this, but you can make other kinds of cookies if you prefer. Spread out the cookie dough on a counter, then take cookie cutters and/or a butter knife and cut all kinds of different, but interlocking shapes out the dough. Bake all the shapes, then lay them out on the counter to see how the "puzzle pieces" turn out. After everyone has had the opportunity to admire your work, let the family eat it for dessert!

Help me remember that my life is like a puzzle in your hands, Lord, one that you put together piece by piece with expert care and loving concern.

Daydream

Sit back, relax, and let your mind wander. Imagine what it would be like if you got the dream job, if Martians visited Earth, if you could predict the future, and more. (Umm, if you can predict the future, can you let us know whether or not people will like this book? Thanks.) Daydreaming works particularly well if you add these ingredients: a warm spring day, a comfy hammock, a tall glass of lemonade, and the sound of children playing nearby.

Heavenly Father, let me dream your dreams; then give me the courage to follow those dreams to accomplish your purpose.

315
Bend the Rules

Yes, we know, every rule has a reason. But we also know that save for God's divine commands, every rule also has an exception. Make an exception to a family rule just for today. Let the boys wear a cap at dinner, keep everyone up late just for fun, go ahead and watch an extra half-hour of TV, and let the dog lick the plate. While you're at it, take the day off from work—just because!

Father, grant us wisdom to correctly balance discipline and freedom in our family.

316
Play "Demolition Derby" with Hot Wheels™

Gather your family and form two teams. Position teams at opposite ends of a hallway, and give each team a handful of toy racing cars. Then, let the derby begin! Take turns rolling your cars toward the center of the hallway, with the aim of making the cars "crash" in the middle. Count how many rolls it takes until two cars actually hit each other, see if you can get a four-car collision going, and for the last round, send all cars flying down the hall at once! (Warning: If your teenager seems a wee bit too enthusiastic about this idea, you may want to hide the car keys for a while.)

Help us all, Lord, to drive and walk safely.

317

Give Yourself a Sunscreen Tattoo

It's true. If you put sunscreen on your body in certain designs, then lie out long enough to get a tan, you can create a temporary "tattoo" of lighter color skin in the area where you applied the sunscreen. Think of the possibilities. You could sunscreen Superman's "S" on your chest, put your favorite Bible reference on your arm, and more. Design your own "tattoo" on paper first, then practice making the design with lotion on your skin. When you're ready, grab a bottle of sunscreen and go get a tan!

Jesus, let your love mark our lives.

318

Make a "What I Like about Me . . . " List

Several years ago the Romantics had a hit song called "What I Like about You." We figure you should be ready just in case they decide to write a new song called "More Stuff I Like about You" in the near future. Take out a pencil and a pad of paper and list all the things there are to like about you. For starters, there's the fact that you are loved by God, that you have a great sense of humor, and that you're reading this book! Now, you go ahead and finish your list. Take as long as you like, we'll be here when you get done.

Thanks for liking me more than I even like myself, Jesus.

319

Mix Ethnic Flavors to Create a New Food

The world needs a new entrée, and you can provide it. Experiment with ethnic foods to create a unique—and tasty—combination. Try your hand at things like taco pizza, polish-sausage burritos, Italian egg rolls, and quiche pita sandwiches. If you come up with something special, open up a specialty fast-food restaurant and feed it to the world!

Father, help us celebrate the diversity you've created in our world.

320

Make a Sandwich with as Many Layers as You Have Family Members

Gather your family in the kitchen, slap a loaf of bread on the counter along with all your favorite sandwich fixings, and build a multidecker dream sandwich! Add one layer for each family member, and let each person choose what goes in his or her layer. When it's done, slice up enough for everyone to have some and eat up! (If it's really good, add it to the menu of your fast-food restaurant you're creating from creative spark #319.

Jesus, help us always appreciate the unique contributions each one of us makes to our family.

321

Change the Buttons on the Car Stereo

Clear all the preset stations on the car stereo and reprogram them to tune in stations your family normally would never listen to. Try the opera station, the rap station, the 24-hour polka-music station, the news channel and more. Leave these new stations on the car stereo for at least a week. Afterward, discuss these questions: What did we learn about our family's radio choices? If we were to keep one of these new stations on a preset button, which would we be most likely to keep?

Expand our horizons just a bit this week, God.

322

Swap Dinner with Another Family

Enlist another family you trust to join you in this creative spark. Have each family prepare a full dinner and plan to have both dinners ready at an appointed time. When dinner is ready, pack it all up and send it over to the other family for them to enjoy, and have them do the same for your family. Don't tell each other what you're having, just switch dinners sight unseen and let the crescent rolls fall where they may!

For this food we are about to eat, we thank you O Lord.

323
Go on a Blind Date

It's not as bad as it sounds . . . Well, OK, it could be, but think of the fascinating stories you'll have to tell your grandchildren years from now! Make a deal with your best friend that you'll each fix the other up with a blind date. Make it a double date with your friend just to make it less stressful. Then play matchmaker and find each other an escort that could become the person of your dreams! When the date is finished, go home and write down how the whole evening went. Spare no details. After all, your future grandchildren will want to know it all!

Jesus, help me to treat my date the way you would treat that person if you were in my place.

324
Host a Foreign Exchange Student

Check with your local school district to find out about the foreign exchange programs in your area. Volunteer to host a student from another country. Keep a family diary of what happens when your two cultures meet on your home grounds. Try some food from your student's home country. Take your student sightseeing. Ask your student what he or she has heard about the United States and Americans, and why he or she was willing to go so far away from home. Afterward, ask yourselves: If our family were to spend an extended period of time outside the U.S., where would we go? What would we want to do there?

Lord, help us be kind to all people, including those who are different from us.

325
Switch Beds for a Night

Yours is lumpy anyway, right? Just for one night, have every family member switch beds. (You can keep your own pillow, though.) The next morning swap stories about how well you did (or didn't!) sleep in a new setting. Now that you've all tested each other's beds, decide who really has the best mattress, then go ahead and try out creative spark #286.

Jesus, let us rest easy in the comfort of your love tonight.

326
Send a Message in a Bottle

Messages in bottles are the stuff that adventures are made of, so why not give away an adventure to a stranger? Take an empty plastic bottle, write an encouraging note addressed to "Whoever Finds This Bottle," and send it on its way. Now, don't promise any buried treasure or say you've been taken hostage, but just write a note wishing the finder a brighter day. If you like, include a dollar with your note as a small "treasure," and be sure to ask the finder to recycle the bottle if possible!

Share a secret message of encouragement with me today, too.

327
Read a Play in Your Living Room

Get several copies of a favorite play (check with your library or an English teacher to locate enough copies). Then, over the course of several evenings, read the play aloud at home. Have each family member read one or more roles, as necessary, and recreate (without scenery or props) the entire play in your living room. Encourage exaggerated voice characterizations and stay in character for the whole reading. Afterward ask yourselves: Who really brought a character to life during our reading? How did he or she do that? What can we learn from our experience about exercising our imaginations?

Use us to add new drama and excitement to those we meet this week, Creative Spirit.

328

Change Your Clothes after Every Meal

OK, people might think you're a little weird, but that's part of the fun of this spark idea! Tomorrow, plan three outfits to wear instead of just one, and put on a new outfit after every meal. (Depending on the day you do this, you might need to carry a set of clothes along to school with you.) See how many people notice your changes, and take note of which outfit gets the most compliments!

Thank you, Jesus, for being the same yesterday, today, and tomorrow.

329

List Everything New You Learn in a Day

They say you learn something new every day—so let's see if it's true. Take a notepad with you wherever you go today, and each time you notice that you've learned something new, make a note of it on your pad. Spot a shortcut to work? Jot it down. Notice a new way God is working in your life? Add it to your list. Finally, discover the difference between meiosis and mitosis? Write it in your notes. At the end of the day, gather the family together to compare your lists to see who learned the most!

Father, let us learn anew the power of your love in our lives.

330

Sleep In

Turn off the alarm, unplug the phone, draw the curtains and snooze away. First one out of bed is a rotten egg!

Thank you, God, for the gift of rest!

331

Brainstorm Everything Your Family Can Do
that Others Can't

Discover all the really important things that make your family unique. Can you all whistle through your teeth? Quote every line from *The Princess Bride*? Sing all the words (in unison) to "Conjunction Junction" from *Schoolhouse Rock*? Win every egg toss competition at church picnics? Make this list? Post the results of your brainstorming proudly on your bathroom wall—'cause that's another thing only your family can do!

You've made us special, Father, and we give you praise for that!

332

Ask for Autographs after a High-School Event

Practically every hall-of-famer once played high school ball, gold-record artists could be singing in the school chorus, and future Oscar winners might be performing on your high school's stage. Make a bet on the future of the kids in your community (and build their self-esteem at the same time) by collecting autographs of high school performers. Tell them you're making an investment that you hope will pay off when they make the big time. (Plus, this is a good excuse to go to all those activities going on at the high school!)

Use me to encourage someone today, O God.

333

Go to the Circus

The circus is where imagination has run amuck! So get in on the action by taking the whole family out when the circus comes to town. Try to spot the most outlandish costume. Cheer the dare-devils. Laugh with the clowns. Hold your breath during the lion-tamer act. Imagine what it would be like to join the circus, and think about what kind of act you'd most want to perform if you could. (And go ahead and feast on the cotton candy—the clown told us it's a no-calorie kind!)

Let us have good clean fun today, God.

334

Invent a Circus Act

Now that you've seen the real thing, imagine the ringmaster calls with this message: "We accidentally left an act back in Raton! Quick, we need your family to fill in!" What will your family do? Juggle socks? Perform cartwheels and somersaults? Create a human pyramid? Decide a fun act you all can participate in, then work up a 15-minute routine. After all, you never know what might get left behind at the McDonald's in Raton, New Mexico!

Let us make our own good, clean fun today, God!

335

Set Up a Carnival in Your Yard

Just in case you're wondering, it's really a big pain to run away and join the circus. So, if you can't perform under the big top, do the next best thing: Set up a carnival in your backyard! Have booths for things like a cakewalk, beanbag toss, and dropping clothespins in a milk bottle. Have a juggling competition to see who can juggle the most items and who can juggle the longest. If you did creative spark #334, exhibit your talents for the neighborhood. When it's all done, invite Mom and Dad to clean up the mess for you!

Thank you for allowing us to share good clean fun with others, God!

336
Play Do-it-Yourself Miniature Golf

It's true, sometimes going out for a game of miniature golf with friends can be hard on the wallet. Thankfully, you can set up your own do-it-yourself putt-putt course anyplace you've got a lawn! Take a few glass tumblers and lay them out at various places on the lawn—these become the holes. Throw in a few twigs and rocks for obstacles. Then use a wiffle bat for a club and Ping-Pong balls for golf balls (or something else comparable), and challenge your friends to a tournament on your homemade course. (Tell them since you made the course, you get five free strokes during the game!)

Lord, you are more precious to me than a hole-in-one!

337
Put on a Taffy Pull

Grab a book of candy recipes from the library and find the best taffy recipe available. Then invite another family to join yours for a good, old-fashioned taffy pull! Create wacky flavors (like garlic taffy), work in pairs to see who can pull the longest strand of taffy, and combine your candy pieces to make inventive shapes (like a two headed llama!). If you do this around the end of October, make a double batch and give out homemade taffy to trick-or-treaters in your neighborhood when they come by.

Make our lives sweet like candy to those we contact this week.

338
Build a Fort over the Clothesline

With your parents' permission, fold the sheets over the clothesline and stretch out the ends until they touch the ground and form a tent shape. Use bricks or rocks to anchor the ends of the sheet to the ground. Hang towels to make tent flaps—and presto! Your own backyard fort! Take a few toys out there, and maybe a book or two, and spend the next hour or so in the coolness of the damp tent imagining you're stranded on a desert island. (If you want to get on Mom and Dad's good side, offer to rewash the sheets when you're done!)

God, you are a strong and mighty tower for me, a place of refuge for all the days of my life.

339

Listen to a Thunderstorm

Next time God treats your family to a thunderstorm, don't let it go unnoticed. Gather everyone near a window or under a shelter outside and spend a few moments listening to the sounds of the storm. Brainstorm sound comparisons such as "The thunder sounds like a giant roaring," or "The rain sounds like the foot-steps of a thousand little people." When you're ready, ask your-selves: What's one interesting thing we might of missed if we hadn't taken time to listen to this storm?

Jesus, thank you for always listening to us during the storms we face in life.

340

Get Blender-Happy

It's amazing what a blender can do, and how many different things taste good once they're combined in a blender. Get blender-happy today and see if you can invent some new, winning combination. Choose four or five things you really like to eat, add water and a few ice cubes, and throw it all in the blender. Let it go until everything is fully liquefied, then taste it! Add other flavors and spices until you get just the right mixture—then offer it as a new health-food drink!

Lord, teach us to blend good things in new ways.

341
Have a Theme for the Day

Add new pizzazz to an average day by creating your family's own theme days. You might try a "Chocolate Day," when you eat at least one bite of chocolate at every meal. Or you could have a "When Parents Were Kids Day" and dress in styles from the parents' youth and participate in some form of entertainment popular from that time. Or you might have an "I Love You Day," when everyone expresses love for each other in at least three creative ways. Work together to choose a theme, then have fun!

Jesus, no matter the theme for our day, help us make you the theme for our lives.

342
Tape Your Face into Funny Expressions

Don't worry, as long as you don't tape your nose, mouth, or eyes shut, this isn't dangerous. Get creative with tape and turn yourselves into a family of silly-faced people. Tape your nostrils up into a pig nose, gather the skin on your cheeks to create new wrinkles, tape one eyebrow higher than the other, tape your wrinkles back into a mock facelift, and so on. When everyone has a fun Scotch-taped face on, take a picture. Bring it out later whenever your family seems overly serious.

Let our faces express the joy of knowing you this week, dear God.

343
Invent a Secret Handshake

Pretend you and your family are undercover spies who dare not be detected by those in the outside world. The only way anyone can enter your home is by revealing they are part of your network by knowing *the secret handshake.* Work together to invent that handshake, and use it as the "key" to enter your house for a week. (If you invite guests over, make sure they know the handshake as well!)

Thank you, Lord, that family members can also be friends!

344

Make a 3-D Picture out of Salad Ingredients

The great thing about this creative activity is you can eat it when you're done! Arrange lettuce, celery, carrots, tomatoes, cucumbers, and other salad ingredients to lay out a 3–dimensional picture on the counter. How about a portrait of Mr. Lettucehead and his carrot eyes? Or a celery boat riding a cucumber tidal wave? Display your artwork for the family at dinner.

Let your creativity flow through us today, dear Father.

345

Play Critic for a Day

Can you believe people actually get paid to write their opinions about movies, music, books, and more? So, just in case you want to be ready to earn a few bucks when the opportunity arises, play "Critic" for a Saturday. Get a new CD, then spend your morning listening to it and writing down what like and dislike about it. Next, go to an afternoon movie. Take notes in the dark briefly describing the movie's plot and rating the acting, story, and special effects. Finally, spend the evening curled up with a book. When you finish it, write your reactions to it. Type everything up, edit it down to about one page for each product, and share it with family and friends.

Help me see, God, the places in my own life that need improvement as well.

346
Indulge in a Bubble Bath

Life's too short not to enjoy its little indulgences. Send all the kids to Aunt Sandra's and spend some private time in a bubble bath to make Robin Leach jealous. Make the water just the right temperature, and go heavy on the bubbles and perfume-scented soaps. Add classical music playing on the stereo, a platter of cheese and crackers, and sparkling cider served in chilled glasses. Then relax and enjoy!

Jesus, thank you for a chance to relax today.

347
Create a Family Art Gallery

Clear out space on one wall in your home and designate it as your Family Art Gallery. Let each family member contribute one piece of artwork to display for the world in this personal gallery—pictures from school, clay models on a small shelf, doodles you particularly like, unique photographic collages, and so on. Make it a rule that each family member can display only one art piece at a time, and encourage everyone to change their displays from time to time just as they would in a professional art gallery.

Let our lives be on display for you, dear God.

348
Let Your Fingers Do the Walking through a Fabric Store

Take a family excursion to a nearby fabric store and let your fingers do the walking down the aisles. Compare the textures of the various fabrics to find the consensus picks in the following categories: Roughest, Softest, Most Like Mom's Favorite Sweater, Best for a Plush Animal, Most Like a Cloud, Most Like Our Living Room Curtains, Our Family's Personal Favorite. Remember, make your judgments by touch only, not by color or pattern!

Thank you, Father, for the gift of touch.

Imitate Kermit the Frog in Every Conversation Today

"Kermit the Frog here!" Did we fool you? Yes, we know. We sound just like him, huh? (We've practiced for years.) Now, you don't have to fool anybody, just talk in a Kermit-like voice at least once in every conversation today. See if you can get somebody else to imitate Grover or Cookie Monster or Miss Piggie.

Give me the grace to imitate you best of all, Jesus.

350

Be Spontaneous

So what if the kids are ready for bed and Mom and Dad have settled in to read the evening paper? There's ice cream to be had out there! Jump in the car in your pajamas for a visit to the local ice cream palace. Or why not take a wrong turn just to see where it takes you? Or quit working and schoolwork long enough to play a game just because it sounds like fun? It's spur-of-the-moment times like these your family will remember a lifetime, so take advantage of the creative breaks you discover in a day—whether you're ready for them or not!

Make us ready and willing to follow you at a moment's notice, dear God.

351

Host a "Favorite Children's Book" Party

Invite two or three other families over, and require each person attending to bring his or her favorite children's book as admission to the party. (If you want, you can have people dress up as characters from their chosen books.) Sometime during the party have guests take turns telling why the books are their favorites and reading the books aloud to each other. See how many new books you discover during the party. After the party vote on who read his or her story with the most enthusiasm and characterization.

Lord Jesus, help us to value childhood as much as you do.

352

Carve a Basket out of a Watermelon

Hone your fruit carving skills with this spark. (If you become a world-famous banquet chef because of this creative spark idea, be sure to invite us to dinner!) Use a carving knife (carefully!) to sculpt the form of a basket and handle out of the watermelon's oval shape. Scoop out the meat of the melon in balls, and refill the basket with them. Include other fruit in your basket such as strawberries and pineapple, and serve it all to your family as a special treat for dinner. (Inform them that applause and profuse thanks are welcome!)

Holy Spirit, let your fruits of joy and peace show in my life today.

353

Tie a Flashlight to Your Shoe and Go for a Night Hike

OK, so it's not exactly in the Boy Scout manual, but it does light up your path at night! See how aiming your light with your feet affects your ability to move in the darkness. Does it make it easier or harder for you? What do you notice that you might have otherwise missed? What do you miss that you normally would have noticed? If you want to make it really difficult, tie the flashlight so the beam shines behind you, then walk backwards all the way home!

Lord, help us to use your Word to light the paths we take in life.

354

Revise the Federal Tax System

Hey, somebody's gotta do it. Who knows, with the right idea you could run for President of the United States. (If you win, remember to invite us for a personal tour of the White House!)

God, grant the leaders of our country the wisdom and desire to accomplish your will in our government.

355
Blow Bubbles

Mix dish soap with water and begin this adventure! See how many different things you can use to blow bubbles with (such as a straw, the tube from a roll of paper towels, a ring, a washer, your fingers curled in a circle, an empty thread spool, a hula hoop, as well as the traditional bubble wand). See if you can blow a bubble that stays intact at least 10 seconds. Try blowing a bubble within a bubble, or the largest bubble, or the smallest bubble. Afterward, put on a Bubble Show to exhibit your newfound talents for your family.

Father, help me accomplish more than I ever thought possible in life by always trusting in your power within me.

356
Visit the Places Where You Were Born

Take the family to check out the actual buildings (or cabs!) in which you were born. You may need to drive past old homes, tour a hospital or two, or view a vacant lot where a doctor's office once stood. Imagine how each location has changed and see what has stayed the same. If you were born in places far away from where you live now, plan a vacation or two that takes you to attractions near your birth sites. (Those trips take our family to California, Virginia, and Oklahoma!)

Jesus, help us remember where we came from as we keep our hearts focused on where we're going—heaven.

357
Break a World Record

Check out the *Guinness Book of World Records* from your local library, and begin looking through it to find that one record you think you can break. Can you shoot free throws without missing? Build the tallest sandwich in the world? Eat more pizza than the record holder? Why not give it a try? And if you can't find a record to break, invent one. (For example, you could always set a record for being the first person in your house to sit on an omelet!)

In all that I do, may I give glory to you, O Lord.

358

Collect One Souvenir from Every State in the Union

You'll have to be opportunistic and inventive for this spark. As a family, work together to see how long it takes for you to collect one souvenir from every state in the U.S.A. Have friends send you postcards, pick up trinkets on business trips or vacations, send for information from Chambers of Commerce, and more. Keep everything on a shelf in your home, and label which state each item is from. When you finally collect that 50th object, go to a baseball game, sing heartily the "Star-Spangled Banner," and eat apple pie!

Thank you, dear God, for allowing us to live in a country like ours.

359

Play Fetch with the Ocean

Next time you visit the beach, look for a piece of driftwood about the size of your hand and use it to play "fetch" with the ocean. Toss that driftwood as far into the surf as you can, then watch for it to reappear on the shore when the waves wash it in. It may come right back to your feet, or it may drift down the beach a bit, so keep a keen eye out for it! See if you can go the whole day without losing your wood, then take it home and save it for your next trip to the beach.

No matter how far I may stray, Lord, please keep drawing me back to you.

Play "TV Theme Song Trivia"

Pick up a TV-theme-song CD from your local library or music store, then bring it home to test your family's knowledge of TV music. Gather around the stereo and designate one person as the "CD Spinner." The rest are "Experts." Play the beginning of a song, then allow Experts to make their guesses as to the TV show to which the song belongs. Play as long as you like, taking turns being the CD Spinner and the Experts. If you get really good, challenge another family to take you on at "TV Theme Song Trivia!"

Our loving Father, let us become experts at loving each other.

361

Write the Ending of a Sitcom

Yes, it's true that most TV sitcoms are predictable and trite. That's why they need you! Together with your family, watch the first 15 minutes of a sitcom, then turn off the TV. Have your family brainstorm at least five possible endings for the show. (Of course, your endings will be better than the real thing anyway!)

Creative God, let our imagination run wild—and our joy run free.

362

Ride Along with a Police Officer

Many local police forces offer what they call "ride-alongs" for local citizens. That means they allow you to ride along as an observer with an officer on his or her shift. Call your local police station to inquire about this program and to make the necessary arrangements. When you go on your ride-along, take a journal and jot quick notes or thoughts that come to you during the shift. Later, answer these questions: What's one new thing I learned about police work tonight? How will that change the way I view police officers in the future? Be sure to send a thank-you note to the police station afterward.

Jesus, please keep the police officers in my city safe from harm and help them do their jobs to the best of their abilities.

363

Go Behind the Scenes

Have you ever noticed that classes of young children get to go on the coolest tours? When our son was in little, he toured the post office, a farm, an air-traffic control tower, a tea factory, a publishing company, an ice-cream shop, and more. Why not arrange a behind-the-scenes family tour instead of a classroom tour? Make a list of all local businesses that your family would be interested in touring, then call to see if they'd allow your family a behind-the scenes glimpse at how they work. (Don't forget to ask for souvenirs at the doughnut shop!)

Thank you, Jesus, for all the people who get things done but never get much credit for it.

364

Give a Gift for No Reason at All

Who says there must be a reason for a gift? It doesn't have to be Christmas to share a little of God's love to others, so go ahead and give today. How about a hug for your parents? or a small toy to a friend? or a service of doing a chore for your brother or sister? or a drawing for your grandparents? See if you can give one present of some kind to at least five people today—just for no reason at all!

Father, thank you for the greatest gift of all—your son, Jesus.

365

Send Us Your Best Creative Spark
That's *Not* in This Book!

Mail it to: Mike & Amy Nappa, c/o Augsburg Fortress Publishers, Box 1209, Minneapolis, MN 55440. We look forward to hearing from you!

Dear Jesus, please grant the family of Mike and Amy Nappa an abundance of your grace, peace, and joy.

366

Treat Yourself

You deserve it!

Dear Jesus, please grant our family an abundance of your grace, peace, and joy as well!